Show Them Through Me

Unfiltered Grace

Chris Annette Smith

The Grace Collective Publishing

SHOW THEM THROUGH ME

Published by The Grace Collective Publishing Royal, Arkansas

The events and experiences in this book are true to the best of the author's recollection. Some names and identifying details have been changed to protect the privacy of individuals.

Cover artwork by Melissa Perrigo
Cover design by The Grace Collective Publishing

For my mom, who left the suitcase and the secrets for me to find when I was finally strong enough to carry them. I hope I told our story with the grace you deserved.

"If I find in myself a desire which no experience in this world can satisfy, the most probable explanation is that I was made for another world."

— C.S. Lewis, *Mere Christianity*

CHAPTER 1

Hi. My name is Chris. It's not Christine or Christie. It's just Chris and I'm a girl, not a boy. When I was a kid snooping through old boxes one time, I found an old envelope where my mom had slid her finger underneath the flap to tear it open and pulled out the bill that was probably inside. Most likely long after the bill had been forgotten or paid, she tore the short sides of the envelope and unfolded it into a tattered square.

She used a black pen and drew a line down the middle of the paper, making two columns of prospective baby names for me. In the first column she wrote Diane with a line drawn underneath. In the second column she wrote Frank and drew a line underneath. In the first column was written Chris in her very neat and perfect cursive and in the second column my dad had scrawled out Christine and Christie alongside some doodles and scribbles. Next to that, in his handwriting, he wrote my middle name, Annette.

I always wanted my mom to be the one that wanted to name me Christine or Christie, but that is not how it was. She wanted me to have a boy's name. At least that's what I always accused her of. Maybe that's why when I was younger he would be the hero in the stories my mind would tell me because he picked my middle name that was supposed to go with my real name, but somehow I didn't get my real name.

It was my mom who insisted that my name be Chris. My name. It tortured me. It was the first thing I wanted to change about myself. Unfortunately, the only part of changing my name that I was good at was my last name.

I wasn't trying to get good at it. I was just trying to just have a good life.

By the sixth time, I decided to step off the trail of marriages and mistakes and decided to give myself back the name I was originally given when I came into the world. I was this close to finally erasing 'Chris', but ultimately I couldn't think of a better name to describe this mess than Chris.

My dad must not have cared if she gave me a boy's name or not because he already knew my nickname was going to be "Sissy". The problem was, nicknames only stick if there's someone around to call you that. He moved us away from everyone that would call me that. I thought maybe if he'd have known how it would all turn out, he would have tried harder to get his way with naming me.

I had penpals that I would write and just so there was no mistaking that I was a girl, as if my handwriting in purple ink on pink papers weren't enough, I would sign my name "Christie" instead of Chris. My mom hated it. It was like a dig to her every time I would get a letter addressed to "Christie Burkett." Forty years later, I am reminded that I did that to her when I get an email addressed to "Mr. Smith" .

I used to look in the mirror and ask myself, "don't you know who I am?" I don't ask myself that anymore. After forty some odd years of asking, this book emerged and then I finally really started figuring out the answer. I'm Chris. Not Christine, not Christie, and certainly not Mr., but just Chris. It's what made me finally realize exactly who I am. It was so dang simple the entire time. My name. Chris. That's who I am. I am simply "one who carries Christ."

It sounds holy, doesn't it? But for a long time, I felt less like a carrier and more like a graveyard.

I loved my middle name more than I hated my first name. What she did to me with my first name, she redeemed herself by letting me have my middle name. Annette. There were days when that name let me day dream and know that she didn't mean me any harm by giving me a boy's name.

When I started out writing this book, I thought I was going to tell you how crazy my mom was and what a crazy life she had and how crazy my life was because of her. What I realized was that I am only as crazy as I allowed myself to believe that I am. I don't know how crazy my mom actually was. At times I think she let her mind run away with her because it was too hard to fight the voices in her head telling her lies. What I do know is that had I not listened to a sermon when I was seven, she might have really lost her mind.

I spent many, many years preaching that sermon to her, reminding her that it was up to us to decide what we think about. One tiny thought can become huge. The more times you go back and revisit those thoughts they become obsessions. If I keep going back to revisit that thought knowing I shouldn't it can lead to me questioning my own intelligence and sanity.

There were many times my mom told me that she knew she was retarded and nobody wanted to tell her the truth.

Now I know that most likely she was going through a season of despair. I was there when she came out of those seasons as well. When I have sat and thought back about those times, I can compare it to seeing her picking herself up, dusting herself off and standing up straight to shine bright like a light again.

Of course I can't look back without seeing all the things I could have changed and all the things I regret. When I get to those places I can almost vividly remember weighing the pros and cons. When I was younger I didn't purposely make her life harder, but I played a big part in making her life harder because I was trying to make 'adult' decisions with a child's heart.

I used the logic I'd picked up from sermons and books to weigh pros and cons, trying to navigate a house that was burning down. Well, to the best of my ability and understanding depending upon the age I was. I started living this way from the time I could begin halfway comprehending what I was reading.

My dad taught me to read when I was three. Most likely on a bet that someone else thought it couldn't be done. I memorized every word in the book and as soon as my little brother turned three, I started teaching him to read the same book. I figured it was the least I could do since my dad couldn't do it himself. As much as it made her life harder, I'm sure at times it played a big part in making her life much easier.

My goal was to honor my mother and God as my father the very best I could so that I could live a really long time on earth. Even at five, I knew that was harder done than said. There were things she did and things she let happen that I didn't understand, but I didn't question because she was my mother and I vowed to obey her the best I could.

It was easy in the beginning of my life because there weren't very many angry bits, just alot of sad bits and I understood all too well very young what it was like to be so sad about your life because I laid next to the only adult I had in my life while she cried herself to sleep.

The phrase "everything works together for good" was something repeated to me over and over as a child so much so that as an adult, I knew it was a significant part of who I am. The belief that everything does work together for good. The first part of that comes from the scripture that keeps me holding on to life when all I want to do is let go and give up. Every time I would recite it to my mother, most likely when I was trying to convince myself there was still hope by saying it outloud, she would then say, "to them that love the Lord and are called according to His purpose and you, my daughter, are called according to His purpose."

There were times my soul would cringe at the sound of the words "to them that love the Lord." It was at those times I was so far from the definition of a perfect daughter that it didn't matter if I loved the Lord or not, I was pretty sure He couldn't even tell, even if I said I did. There are times that I can still hear her voice in my head, reciting to me those same words. Many of those times I'm struggling trying to figure out "His purpose" because most of the time I have absolutely no idea what He could possibly want with somebody like me, especially on one of my bad days.

The bad days were really dark when I felt I had nothing else left to lose that could make me feel any worse than I already did. The reason I could hold on was because my life had always been a testimony of good things coming from bad things. I have always had absolutely no doubt that something good would come of the worst of the worst situations.

Some situations have taken being away from them for forty years to see the good that came out, but He never gave up on me finding it.

Even if no one else could believe it, because they couldn't see it and the waiting sometimes seems to take forever, I still believed it. I had seen it happen time and time again and I had no doubt that my life would change again for the good and that good things would come from anything meant to make my life look like it had no value.

I was raised to see the good in things even when I was suffering. Sometimes I think I might seem a little jaded or have a morbid sense of humor, but sometimes you have to make a little light of the situation in order to see past the shadows. When I've invited myself to my own pity party, the only way I can leave is to try to see the situation or trial or time of suffering, whatever you want to call it, from a perspective that's not my own, but God's. When I look at things from His perspective, He takes in the whole picture and sees how things affect everyone around me, not just me. My suffering taught me how to look for Him in things that are hard like sickness, hurt, pain, and the even harder things like abuse, broken hearts and death. Somebody's life changed for the better and most of the time when I'm angry it's hard to be honest and point out the good.

I've never learned how to make the suffering completely stop. I think I keep hoping for the day I can sit before God and there is no more sorrow or tears, but sometimes I don't stop and think long enough to remember that good part is what is coming. That's not how it is right now and that's not going to change. You might catch me on one of my good days and get to thinking my life is always rainbows and sunshine, but I assure you it is not. My life is only good because God is good. All the time. Even on my bad days.

There are still experiences I've been through that left me hurt and still make me twinge. A memory will get stirred up every now and then and sometimes if I look for God there and I let Him, He lays out the whole picture of that particular situation and shows me how He was there the whole time. From the beginning to the end. He didn't leave me then and He's not going to leave me now.

It wasn't until after my mom was gone that I was able to look back and see that even when I thought I was stuck with the most horrible mom ever, truly I was blessed to have such an incredibly strong woman to be my mom. There's a verse in the Bible that says if you look for Him with your whole being you will find Him. I think of it as looking for the hand of God moving in your life by directing you around the paths that would have led you to destruction. I'm not saying that when God moved in my life it was instant happiness. The waiting part for the joy to come after God moved was hard and even now, it's still hard, but so worth it because I have peace and I know that joy is definitely coming.

I started writing this very book at a time when I was sitting in a very dark moment, holding on for dear life to a Father I couldn't see, waiting for the good to appear. Honestly, I never saw it like that then. I saw it as a "screw this. I'm done. The relationship I was in at the time made it seem like all I did was work for someone else's enjoyment even though I had most everything anyone could want in life. A nice house, a nice car, nice clothes, and plenty of food. I had hobbies that included good friends and expensive accessories. I traveled more than most people I knew.

It was the kind of picture perfect life just like you see in magazines, technically beautiful, but entirely staged. The smiles were just muscles holding a pose until the camera clicked. I finally told myself, "Anything is better than this, even if I have nothing."

There were so many feelings and memories that I had stashed away because I didn't want to deal with it at the time. I heard someone say once, "you can't or you won't?" I kept telling myself the day would come that I would sit down and take a good look at all the memories I had stashed in there and then I would carefully fold them all back up and pack them all back away. Every time I thought that day had come, I couldn't do it and even if I could, I wouldn't. I had too many people depending on me to risk having a mental breakdown.

Some of those people told me I was just as crazy as my mother. Some of them told me that I would never be anything more than poor, white, trailer park trash. Those people were usually the same people that also confessed their dying love for me in public. Once I finally convinced myself that life alone was better than what I was doing, I didn't care if I broke. I didn't care if they broke. I was already in pieces, and frankly, an empty house was starting to look like a better place to be. I was done. My life had to change.

CHAPTER 2

I didn't realize it when it started, but each time my feelings got hurt, I would dismiss it because I thought it wouldn't happen again. Each time I dismissed the hurt feelings, I thought I was forgiving and maybe I was, but eventually I had no more forgiveness in me or maybe I just couldn't forgive anymore. All I knew was that I had been the one who had taken the blame and was being punished for things that I didn't do for long enough.

The truth of it was I was the one who would start treating everyone else as though they needed to pay for the wrongs someone else had done to me and by the time I figured that out, I was almost fifty years old. I had been carrying around most all of the wrongs that had been done to me since I was the baby in the belly of my mother while she sat and scratched out on that piece of old envelope paper what my name would be.

Even the covenant marriage I thought was so real, was just an illusion. Not even a double promise could keep out temptation and when I figured that out, I also figured out that I didn't even have to choose spirituality or legalism to get out of my relationship. Either way I got to walk away. I thanked God that He gave me what I thought was a spiritual and legal loophole to rescue me from that situation.

Figuratively and literally I stamped "VOID" over the past fifteen years and started looking ahead to the future.

So there I was. I was sitting there feeling like my suitcase had just exploded. It was the one that I had packed full of every unwanted memory. It was so full that there was no room left for the last fifteen years of bad memories I was hanging on to that I needed to be shoved in there. I wanted to do what I always did and put on a brave face in spite of my life being turned upside down. I wanted my life to look picture perfect, just like what everyone else's life looked like to me. Most of all I didn't want to look like a failure.

My call of desperation was usually preceded by me telling myself, "when you make messes, you like to make them big, don't ya?" This particular time I had messed up big because I decided to make this life changing decision right before I was supposed to run a 100k (about 62 miles) race that I had trained for harder than anything else I'd ever trained for in my life.

After my mom passed away, I decided to take up running. It started with just wanting to get into shape and feel better, but it progressed to running races and finding friends that also were runners. It wasn't long before years had gone by and I had run numerous 5k races, followed by Half Marathons, Full Marathons and then Ultra Marathons which consisted of anything over 26.2 miles. Most of my "training" consisted of running several miles during the week and 20 miles or more on the weekends. I met hundreds of other runners and a select few that gave numerous hours out of many of their days, weeks and months to go out and run with me. There is no doubt that the time they spent with me played a big part in helping me keep my sanity through some tough times.

I'll admit that I usually halfway trained for races. I had moments I had glimmers of hope that I could do better than what I was doing, but most of the time I did just enough to get by. Usually, just finishing the race was good enough for me even though it usually meant I was the last one to cross the finish line. However, this time was different, I had trained so well that my expectations were that I had a chance at finishing and finishing well.

Now that I added even more mental stress on myself, I decided that my goal was just to come in before the cutoff and finish the race. So, at that point, if I came in last in the race, I would be elated just to have the mental and physical endurance to cross that finish line! It felt like all my hopes and dreams were tied up in crossing that line in time. My life up until then had mostly consisted of things I had in the beginning thrown all of myself into, but eventually gave up on because it was too hard. More times than not, it felt like the reason it was too hard was because someone was always trying to steal my dreams and dash my hopes. It was a constant battle of fighting the feeling of being "one-upped" when all I wanted was the satisfaction that I had done my best. It seemed like striving for excellence turned into just trying to survive. I had decided that I was going to try to survive the race long enough to finish and then be done with running and bad relationships once and for all.

I used to jokingly justify that my mess-making abilities were so good because I strived to do everything to the best of my ability. In all seriousness, there were points in my life when people noticed that I wasn't doing everything to the best of my ability and took it as a sign that something in my life was wrong. They asked me about it. Fortunately, instead of reporting me to the authorities, they helped me. Most people I told just enough about the situation for them to leave me alone and not interfere, but that's something I'll tell you about later on in this story.

Before I tell you about finishing the race, first, you have to know where my heart was when I went in it. Not long before race day, I felt like I was sitting in front of my Father looking at flashes of memories from the past that mostly consisted of the giant mess I had created of my life. It was probably a lot like what "your life flashing before your eyes before you die" might feel like without the "before you die" part. I didn't want to die. I was just so embarrassed of what I had become.

I knew my mom expected me to grow up and be a good Christian church girl, but what I thought was her definition of a good Christian church girl, was impossible for me to become. So instead, I became a mixture of who I thought she wanted me to be and who I thought I wanted to be, which I never really knew for sure, and ended up becoming a mixture of a strong "I'll kick your ass" person to some and a somewhat softer and mature voice of reason to others.

Then, I figured out that the real me that lives inside me hadn't matured a bit. I was still the child of an alcoholic father and a mother diagnosed with multiple personality disorder, a child that had been thrust into adulthood way too soon, who had lived alone as a widow at sixteen years of age, divorced more times than I'd like to admit, with enough job history to fill up about twenty pages of a resume (which I've now learned to be proud of), an orphan with no living parents or grandparents and only a handful of family, feeling sorry for myself, asking my Father God to once again show me the good in what was left of the mess I had made of my life.

There had been times before when something would stir up a memory, but as soon as I started to go down Memory Lane, I would stop myself because I knew it would be a long, tearful, heart wrenching trip back home. One memory would lead to another. That memory to the next memory straight past the good that came from my mistakes to the knowing I could've done something different. Then came the questions of, what if I had done something different? What if I had listened to my mom? Then, there I was. I had fallen right into the rabbit hole. I always knew I liked Alice in Wonderland for some reason. I think at times, she knew exactly how I felt.

As I was falling down the rabbit hole and seeing parts of my life flash by, I became angry. I started blaming anyone and everyone I could think of for every time I had gotten a bad deal in life. I thought all the way back to the person who gave birth to me and then suddenly remembered the promise I had made to her to write this book and which I obviously had not followed through. It was then that I finally looked up long enough to realize that ten years had passed by and I didn't have much to show for that promise. Well, nothing except an old yellow worn-out suitcase she left me that I hadn't even opened yet.

Before I tell you about the suitcase, let me tell you what happened at the race. I had always imagined that going into a 62-some-odd-mile race, I would be strong and come out broken down, ready to be rebuilt back even stronger. That seemed to be a pattern in my life. Get broken down, learn from your mistakes, walk away from everything and move forward on to better things.

Actually, with me it was more like light a match, burn it all down and start over.

However, at that point, I was pretty much broken down so far that I decided that the worst thing that could happen was that I would have plenty of time to think. There would be enough time during the race for me to take a serious trip down Memory Lane and then I would finish the race and that would be the end of it. Little did I know it would launch me, or rather hurl me, in the direction I'm going now.

It was February 19, 2022. The day of the Lovit 100k race. I knew the race was going to be physically tough and I was already at a disadvantage because I had skimped on the last few weeks of my training. My mental state was unstable at best. The Tuesday before the race I flipped the trail the bird and said that no one could make me run. By Friday night I was all in and was going to finish even if it killed me. Saturday morning came and I had decided to just do the best I could.

At 6:00 a.m. I heard "GO!" *Dammit, they started without me.* I was only a few feet away from the start line so I ran against the runners who had already started, put my foot over the line and turned around. After about a mile of asphalt we turned and got onto the trail. I just put one foot in front of the other and pretty soon I had settled into a comfortable pace. It wasn't long before the memories started flooding back.

"Let's meet once a month and do something fun. My treat."

"Remember, we are all dying. I just happen to be doing it a little faster than most."

"What if you only had 30 days to live? What would you do? Who would you spend it with?"

She really didn't have much of a choice. I made her spend her last 30 days with me. A few months before she had talked about moving out into her storage shed and letting a homeless person live in her house. The conversation went something like this:

"I need a favor."

"What's that?"

"I need your sister to live with you."

"Why? Is something wrong? Where are you going to live?"

"I'm going to live in the shed outside and let someone that needs a home live in the house."

"Mom, you need a home to live in. That's why you got the house."

"I'll be just fine in the shed, but she can't live inside the house with a homeless person and it's not fair to her to live in the shed with me."

My mom had been renting a house for years when someone told her about Habitat for Humanity. I'm not sure how long it took for someone to convince her to fill out an application, but eventually she did. Over the next several weeks following my mom submitting the application for a house to be built for her, she and I would have several conversations about whether or not she should withdraw her application so someone else could have her house.

Most of those conversations would be me trying to convince her that she was eligible according to their rules. However, one of the rules was that my sister could not live there with her because she was eighteen years old and was employed. Some days my mom was certain that the rule did not apply to her. It's obvious to me now that this was probably the real reason she wanted my sister to move in with me. Maybe she was just trying to come up with a good enough excuse for me to say I would do it and she could still follow the rules.

I, on the other hand, was not a rule follower so I was always able to come up with a logical way for her to skirt around the rules. She had to think about operating in the gray area, which she hated, but she usually backed off and changed the subject for a while. After all, I had made my life difficult enough without trying to take on my sister right then.

She would ask a few more times for me to let my sister move in with me. I knew that eventually she would come live with me after my mom passed, but right then dealing with my mom dying was hard enough. If I threw my sister into culture shock by moving her in with me, my life would be even harder than it already was. So, I did the only thing I knew to do. I kept putting her off and hoped that I was making the best decision for all involved, including my sister. Eventually that obsession or personality finally faded away. It seemed like near the end, one by one the personalities that were left started, well for lack of a better word, dying.

As I drifted in and out of thought I tried to take in all of the beauty of the nature that surrounded me while being assured I was still on the right path. Fortunately, the course was well marked and was complete with plenty of creek crossings and amazing views to take your mind off how much further you had to go. The snow and ice that covered some of the trees and the ground in places was just a bonus distraction. There was a section about 8 miles or so that ran along a ridge. It was a steep climb getting to it, but the view of the lake for the next eight or so miles made every foot of climb worth it.

The majority of the course was single track trail, meaning there was only room for people to go single file, not side by side. Once the race had started, the runners had spread out so that there was so much distance between you and the person in front of you to make you think you were out in the woods all alone at times.

I tried entertaining myself with stories of "What had happened was..." but pretty soon it just got depressing. I started imagining that the trees were people and that became even worse. Finally, I decided I wasn't happy running. I wasn't sure I even liked running anymore. I felt broken down going in and decided at Mile 29 I had gotten my mind and my thoughts straight again and I was done and ready to go back home. It was news to me, but apparently, I was not done yet.

Just prior to the turn around I was told by a running friend that if I quit, they quit.

Not fair, but well played.

At the turn around I was given two shots of blackberry whiskey and a ham sandwich and told to get back out there. Somewhere around mile 33, the opening chords of One Last Breath started to play.

Then the tears came as the words blared through the headphones. *Please come now, I think I'm fallin', I'm holdin' on to all I think is safe, It seems I found the road to nowhere, And I'm trying to escape.*

Not long before she died, my mom and my sister both moved in with me. When her lucid moments were fewer and farther between, I sent her emails to tell her things I wanted her to know in case I wasn't there when she was awake.

One of the emails I wrote said, "Mom, I'm not ready for you to go yet. I finally feel like I have my mom and not just one of the pieces of my mom. There's not enough time left."

Her reply was what only my mother would say, "I love you but not near as much as God does. You are so precious to Him. He will bless you with your heart's desires just like He has blessed me. love, Mom"

About a mile before the next aid station, a friend who had my shared sense of morbid humor, came looking for me and asked how my mom was doing.

"Is she still in the car?"

I said, "Yep."

How she knew exactly what to say I'll just chalk it up to my friend and I must share a little sixth sense as well. After my mom died, I had her cremated. I kept the ashes on a top shelf in my closet for many years. When I moved, I put her on the floorboard of the backseat of my car and just never took her back out. Several of my running friends met my mom's box of ashes and the ones that ran with me got to hear some stories about her every now and then. She is now safely back in my house, somewhere, for those of you that may be wondering. We talked about it before she died and she told me that ending up in my closet was a risk she was willing to take.

As I headed out of the aid station and back onto the trail of the race course, Beautiful Day started to play. *It's a beautiful day, Sky falls you feel like, It's a beautiful day, Don't let it get away.* It wasn't about my past anymore. It wasn't about my future. It was about living in the moment and me finishing this race. It was about proving to myself that I most certainly did have it in me to do this. I was not a victim of my past. I might have tucked a few things away here and there, but I was not broken. I just needed a little patchwork and reinforcement.

I asked her, "Who will pray for me when you're gone?"

I got to Brady aid station and found that my running friend, who threatened to quit if I quit, had asked her pacer to stay and wait there for me instead of going on with her. If I hadn't been so tired, I would have tried to reason with the million questions that tried to start flooding through my head. Instead, I used my strength to concentrate on how grateful I was for her making such a huge sacrifice at the expense of her own race so that I would keep trying to finish mine. I had made it there just before it was getting dark and by this time running was a relative term. We headed out for the hellacious climb to go back up on the ridge I had come down from that morning, but this time there was no view. It was dark and the only light was coming from the lights we wore on our heads.

The clouds had settled on the ridge and snow and sleet had begun to fall. My pacer encouraged me to just run the downhills the best I could to try to make up a little time. My daughter, Marina, sent me a text "Run til you can't, then run a little more!!" I found a little aid station in the middle of the woods. All I had to do now was get to the next aid station to pick up my next pacer. A few miles later I saw a light in the distance coming the wrong way. *Hey pretty lady, you need an escort to the finish?* I was so relieved. What I really wanted was to be carried because by this time my feet were soaked and I was getting blisters. The creek crossings had become too high to cross without getting my feet wet.

"You can do whatever you set your mind to do."

It was one of the last things my mom had told me as she slipped away.

I set my mind to finish and that is just what I did. One last turn onto another muddy trail in the dark and I started to see the lights from the street. I was on my way to the finish line. Finally, not only did I finish, I finished well ahead of my goal. I don't remember saying it and I wouldn't have believed it except there's a video. At the finish line the race director said, “Are you Chris?” My reply was, “Yes. Last I heard.”

It turned out that nineteen hours and twenty some odd minutes of thinking was not nearly enough to fix everything in my life that was broken. However, I knew going in that the worst thing that could happen to me was I would remember things that I didn’t want to remember, but that surely I would come out the other side of the finish line a little stronger than when I started. Maybe I would be strong enough to finally be able to tell the story I promised my mom I would write. Maybe once again, God made everything work together for good.

I crossed that finish line broken, but for the first time in years, I wasn't empty.

I found God out there on the trail. Somewhere between the physical agony of mile 40 and the solitude of the deep woods, He met me. He stripped away the noise, the pretenses, and the lies until there was nothing left but me and Him. I realized that I couldn't outrun my history, but I didn't have to face it alone anymore.

The race didn't just break my body; it broke the chains of fear that had held me for decades.

I stopped reaching for my running shoes and reached for the suitcase.

CHAPTER 3

I had stumbled across the suitcase a few times in the past. The first time I saw it, it was under her bed. I didn't think much of it. My mom kept all kinds of things under her bed. She had cardboard boxes full of cassette tapes and church booklets.

She had one of those exercise rope contraptions that you hooked to your doorknob. It had a pulley system with four stirrups. You would put each hand and foot in a stirrup and pull on the rope. When you pulled on the rope, your foot would come up. Now that I think about it, I'm not sure what the purpose was, but I know it was fun to play with when I was a kid.

Another time I saw the suitcase, it was in the bottom of her closet. She had told me that she had started journaling about her personalities and I knew that she was keeping her journals in the suitcase.

So, I unzipped it real quick and peeked inside. I wasn't sure what peeking inside was going to get me. If it was really journals like she said, I wouldn't have time to sit and read them, but I could look to see if they really were in there.

Sure enough, I saw a bunch of papers she had written on and a yellow piece of construction paper with a crayon drawing of stick people marching with trumpets up to their mouths. The name

"Willie" was printed on it. The next time I saw the suitcase, it was in her outbuilding with a padlock on it.

Not long before she passed away, we talked about the suitcase. We talked about the fact that she had nothing to give as an inheritance. She had lost the inheritance I was supposed to receive from my father passing away and now years and years later, she had nothing more to give me, except for the suitcase. She made me promise not to open it until after she had died and asked me to use the journals to write her story. I promised her that I would.

"I know it's a big ask and if it's too much, I understand."

All she really wanted was peace knowing that she had not lived her life for nothing and that she lived it, every day, to the best of her ability. Actually, all she really wanted more than anything was for people with mental illness to know that God loved them and could still use them even if they considered themselves broken.

I sat there on the floor, staring at the contents of the suitcase. It wasn't just a collection of old papers; it was the autopsy of a life lived in secret.

As I reached for the first stack of documents, the smell of old paper and stale time hit me. I realized I wasn't looking for "*Mom*" in these pages anymore. I was meeting a stranger.

It took the next couple of years for me to even begin to understand what my mom had been trying so hard to tell me. She was adamant about doing everything to the glory of the Lord. It was a huge part of her, all of her. Through writing her story and reading her journals, I began to understand how the things that happened to her made her who she was.

Regardless of which personality she named herself, they were all "*her*".

They were all *my mom*.

The first document took me back to the very beginning, long before I was born, long before the alcohol, the drugs, the fear, or the voices. It started with a girl who had no idea what was coming.

Her name was Dianne Marie Beadle.

This was one of the first journal entries I pulled out of the suitcase.

Dear real me,

Your whole life you've been afraid that you would not be wanted if you let yourself come out of hiding. I think Baby Wonder is cute and I love her, but are you really letting me see the real you, the real me? I know it's hard. And I know you are just so used to staying hid that it seems to be more comfortable.

But life. Breathing. Living. Loving. Feeling. It's got to be better than hiding.

I want to love you unconditionally, but you know I'm frustrated that you keep hiding. I'm frustrated that you draw pictures I don't understand. If you are the real me, I don't feel connected to you either. There doesn't seem to be an intimate feeling for you.

Sometimes I just look with my mind's eye and think of a little girl whose world came crashing down on her. Whose mommy was too afraid to pick her up. Whose daddy felt love, but couldn't express it.

And she lay wanting to cry, wanting to be held, wanting to talk to someone, wanting someone to talk to her and she left. She left this harsh cruel world.

Diane Beadle – Dear Real Me.

My mom, Dianne Marie Beadle, was born on February 7, 1950 in Washington, Iowa, to my grandmother, Helen Roth, who was not quite 21 years old. My mom was her first child. The way my mom told it, as well as some other family members, was that my grandmother was a nervous wreck and was too scared to pick her up for fear of dropping her or for just plain fear. So even just barely starting out, life was rough for them both. My mom laid in her bassinet all day with a blanket over the top of it waiting. Waiting to be fed. Waiting to be held. Waiting to be changed. Just waiting. I'm pretty sure that's when Baby Wonder or Baby One, as she would call her later, came to be.

She told me that she discovered Baby One during a hypnosis session. Her therapist told her to think back to the very beginning as far back as her memories would allow. I don't know how you get as far back as she did. My own memories start at around three years old, but her memories went back to the time she was an infant. I've never been hypnotized, so I don't know how that works. Since I had never done it, all I could do was to take her at her word.

During her hypnosis session, she remembered all the way back to when she could have only been months, if not weeks old. She was able to see herself laying in a bassinet with a blanket draped over the top. She turned her head back and forth and began to cry. Then she saw a baby looking back at her. The baby was facing her and hovering just underneath the blanket covering the bassinet.

The back of my mom's head was so flat there's no doubt it was from the significant amount of time she spent on her back as a baby. For myself, there's no doubt that Baby One played a key part in my mom's survival. There were times in my own life when the only way out of a situation was for me to take on a persona like someone else, not the real me. I can only imagine that having multiple personalities must be similar only, I knowingly did what I did and remembered doing it. Well, most of the time. There were times I did things that I tried to forget I had done. I guess maybe she could have chosen to not remember the things she wished she hadn't done.

I am not totally convinced that whoever told her initially that she had multiple personality disorder was a believer and I don't think she told her later therapists that she had been diagnosed as having it. Sometimes I think that someone just stuck a label on her to make her doubt her own sanity. It wasn't long after the initial therapist that diagnosed her told her she wasn't making progress and they had done all they could do after she had refused to take the medication they prescribed. She spent the next fifteen years seeing a counselor or therapist on a weekly basis.

In the end it was very necessary for her to see someone. Sometimes I felt like I was her only friend that she confided in, but I had no advice to give when it came to how to deal with some of the bigger questions she had about being married and trying to raise my sixteen year old brother and a little sister who was eleven years younger than him.

She told me once that one of her therapists told her to write letters to her personalities to see if they would write her back. If they could figure out the reason that personality was created, then maybe they could work toward integrating that personality back in with her main personality. Her journal entries were in no certain order, but I'm thinking the journal entry below may have been the first time she tried talking to her personalities.

Dear Personality,

You are hurt and unhappy. Maybe you think no one cares. There are people who care that you are hurt. There is also God's Son Jesus who cares about your hurt. He loves you and can heal your hurting heart. Do you know Jesus?

Love, Mommy

***

Dear Mommy, Jesus can heal my heart? Tell Jesus I'm ugly.

Baby One

***

Dear Baby One,

Jesus knows all about you. He knows you are a beautiful baby. He made you. He saw you in the womb. He understands that you felt unwanted even then. He wants you to know that He wants you. He wanted you for His own glory and He loves you. You were always on His mind. He thought of you continually while you developed in the womb. He thought of you all the days you lay unheld. He knew He would come to you and heal what had been done. He loves you.

Love, Mommy

***

Dear Mommy, I don't have a baby to love. I can't love me I'm not my baby. I have no way to be able to help me. I have no baby. This is my baby. My baby has no way to talk to me. She can't talk to me. I have no baby. I am done talking.

Baby One

***

Dear Baby One,

Do you want to draw a picture? You can draw, but mommy doesn't understand what they mean. Why are you going away?

***

Don't have a way to talk.

***

You can talk with pictures now. I will understand.

***

I went back to bed. I felt uncomfortable. I kept praying questions to God. What shall we do? As I slept I dreamt of a pillow someone was writing on the pillowcase pray. So then I prayed for her. When I awoke I had peace, but also a knowing of Baby One's need. She is so needy. She does not know Jesus. I spent some time in prayer for her this morning and read blessings to her out of God's word. She just watches through my eyes. She wants to believe. She will I feel sure. It may take some time. Her little soul is so hurt. I'm anxious for her to be made whole, but I know we must take time. In the push to be good she left. We must convince her to stay. Not try to compel her to be good. Let her stay just like she is.

When I prayed, I also asked for Jesus to severe the bond between the infant and my Aunt and my Uncle as well as Helen and Bob Roth.

When I awoke I knew why Baby One had written what she wrote. Her mother had flushed her baby down the toilet and so Baby One's baby was down the toilet too. Also, I remembered how fearful my Mom had been when she bathed me. She said she broke out in a cold sweat. She was afraid she'd drop me. She always insists on coming and bathing my babies. I wonder if the curse is not passed on them.

Well, Jesus has come to void out all curses and instead give us a blessing. Me and my household as well.

Diane Beadle 7-30-1995

By this time, I was a young adult in my early twenties. My mom would get so angry with me if I mentioned her mother, Helen, my grandmother. The conversations would usually start as an innocent, non-confrontational question of me asking her how her mother, Grandma Roth as I called her, was doing or if she had heard from her.

Because the conversations usually became tense and ended with my mom taking on some other persona, I tried hard to remember not to ask about my grandmother. Inevitably, missing my grandmother would outweigh remembering who my mom really was and the words would spill out before I could remember that once they were out, I couldn't shove them back in.

At one point my mom was seeing a new therapist, and they convinced her to stop allowing my grandmother, Helen, to call her on the phone, unless my mom had called her first and she was just calling my mom back.

It then progressed to no phone calls at all between them. They would record cassette tapes of them talking to the other, but eventually that too was squashed. It got to where my mom would only allow my grandmother to write her letters and even then, she would only write a letter back to my grandmother if she felt the letter Helen wrote her wasn't spiteful, controlling or manipulative.

It would be enough for me to give up and decide no relationship was better than a relationship with so many rules.

I don't know if my mom ever told my grandmother specifically that she was diagnosed with multiple personality disorder, but I do remember them having a huge disagreement over my mom remembering things that happened to her as a child.

One memory my mom had was from when she was about 4 or 5 years old. She was living with her parents next to a large garden. She had been outside playing and had gotten into a swarm of bees. When she started screaming, my grandmother came running out of the house, saw her covered with bees and stripped all of my mom's clothes off of her right then and there. My mom said that while this was happening there were people working in the garden who had looked up to see what was going on and saw her standing there naked.

When she first told me the story, I thought she was telling me that her neighbors were outside looking at her, but later she told me the story again and with the part of the story my grandmother told me, it apparently was more than just a big garden. The more she described it, it actually seemed to be more like a big field where migrant workers came and worked.

She had also been raised to be extremely modest and you don't dare uncover yourself in public. When she got into the bees, her five-year-old mind couldn't comprehend how you just throw all the rules out the window because you are covered with bees. My five-year-old mom was mortified.

I once thought traumatic events could form individual personalities and that this was how the personality my mom would call Margaret came to be, but I don't think it was just one event that created a personality. My impression is that Margaret came to be over a season of my mom's life, just like with Baby One. It wasn't just the incident with the bees. There were other incidents, probably several more, but most likely it was just the environment that she lived in that happened to create the emotional person she became that she called Margaret.

I raised my children to be modest, but to not be mortified if someone saw them naked. My mom on the other hand was taught when she was little that you keep your dress down, sit with your legs together and don't call attention to yourself.

My grandmother told her this memory never happened, but then said something similar to that may have happened, but it was no big deal and she couldn't believe my mom was making such a huge deal out of it.

I don't recall that she ever mentioned Baby One to my grandmother. I'm sure after telling my grandmother about the incident that created Margaret, it would have been really hard for Baby One to be told it didn't happen and be rejected again.

This was also around the same time my mom had to testify at a trial to defend a man she called her uncle, who was also a leader in her church, who was accused of being inappropriate with another child, from the best that I can make of what I've read. I can only imagine that kind of stress put on a five year old combined with the stress from a situation with the bees would be almost more than a five year old can emotionally take. I have a hard time as an adult being able to emotionally take hit after hit after hit.

Several years before she died, my stepdad, Robert, had died and it was left up to me and my sister to clean out his apartment with a limited amount of time to get it done. It felt like even though his life was over, someone else was pushing me to move his things out of the way because I was holding up someone else moving in and moving on with their life.

In order to keep from going through that again with my mom, I decided to get a head start on it. It wasn't until about ten years after she died that I finally started going through what was left to look at later after packing up her house.

My thinking was that I would deal with the packing part of my mom, then deal with the dying part and then deal with sorting through her things part. When it came time for the sorting through her things part, I sorted things into two categories, things to sell and things to look at later. The things that didn't sell, I took to Goodwill and the things to look at later I put in a mini storage facility so I could look at them later.

The storage facility was locally owned by an older gentleman. When I rented the storage room, he asked me why I needed it and I told him that my mom had died and I needed a place to store her things until I could figure out what to do with them. He was very adamant about the bill being paid on time. Even if I was only a day late, he would start calling me to remind me that I hadn't paid it.

After renting the storage room for a couple of years, I had to make the decision to let it go, along with all of her stuff. I couldn't afford to keep buying more time in order to put off looking at the things to look at later. Pretty soon I had thirty voicemails on my phone letting me know my bill hadn't been paid. Finally, I just made the decision to just let it all go. I gave the owner of the storage room my last payment and told him that I couldn't pay the rent anymore and I just didn't have time to look at it. I didn't want to look at it. I wanted it to just go away and me just accept that I would never know what was really in there. At least, that's what I thought I wanted.

He must have appreciated my honesty and may have even felt a little sorry for me. He told me that he was sorry I had to let it go, but he would take care of getting rid of everything. A couple more years passed and his wife called the office where I worked and said that he had passed away. I told her I used to rent a storage room from them so I was familiar with her husband.

She called me back later that day after she had opened the storage room I used to rent and told me that everything was still there. For some reason he didn't get rid of it like he said he was going to do. She offered to accept payment of $100.00 in exchange for me to come and clear out the storage room.

I went and picked up all of the things that I wanted to look at later.

Still, another couple of years would pass before I would even think about looking in the yellow suitcase or one of the rubber tubs. When I did, I found a large manila envelope in the "things to look at later" full of letters from my grandmother to my mom. In one of the letters dated December 21, 1987, my grandmother wrote:

> *"I have been so concerned about your tape about us breaking Bonds. I have asked the Lord to show me what it is you are wanting to tell me Then I think, is it this or, is it that? I have come to the conclusion that maybe the Lord in You is going to have to tell me, no matter how much it hurts. You know if it's done in a spirit of Love, only healing can come, after the chastisement.*
>
> *I LOVE YOU ALL SO MUCH. I BLESS YOUR NEW YEAR."*

On January 6, 1988, my grandmother wrote:

> *"Your letters are a real blessing to me. I reread the one I received last week end, and also rec. one yesterday, which was a real blessing, especially the drawings. I'm just in alot of "mind" battle at this time, a lot of it gets ministered to me here at the office. Maybe I'm not doing as good as you think about keeping all my bonds broken*

all the time. I may be too open to what's going on here at the office. Anyway, I feel I can be "me" enough to let you know what's happening, so you will realize you're being a blessing to me, and I can't seem to be a blessing back at this time."

Another letter dated February 23, 1988, my grandmother wrote:

"I haven't much to write about. Seems I'm going thru something where the Lord has shut my mouth. I think there must be a scripture that says, "Be still, and learn from me." Matt. 11:29. All I'm doing at this time is presenting myself to the Lord. Rom 12:1. There's only one way I can do it, and that's "by the mercies of God" which is "By the Grace of God."

It was evident in some of the other letters I read from my grandmother to my mom, that my grandmother was trying to right the wrongs my mom felt my grandmother had done to her. The biggest problem my mom told me she had with my grandmother was that my grandmother wanted my mom to quit digging up the past and just let it go. I can understand how uncomfortable it can get when someone won't quit pointing out the stains on the dirty laundry you're trying to wash.

My mom wanted my grandmother to at least acknowledge the past, but my grandmother seemed to be writing about how she felt about that in the letter I found that was written on Thursday, June 23, 1988:

"I got to go to South Gate Saturday P.M. Walter and Cathy took me. Worship was so great. Had a real impartation from the Word Sun. A.M. too. Rick said the word "Worship" means to "prostrate" oneself at his feet. We're still looking up to pull him down and he isn't "up" He's down here. We don't realize we are almost 10 years into the Kingdom. We are into the time of the "Parousia" and it isn't done by willing our minds to worship. Everything we do, if we're walking in submission to Him, is a worship to Him. Another thing he said is, We have no past. As he spoke it, it was imparted, "I have no past." I've got no more points to prove. No more insecurities, no more condemnations. I, by faith, impart that to you. You have no past. God loves you, just like you are. Sure, he's working on us still, but He loves us. You don't have to prove anything to anybody.

I love you too. Bunches and Heaps."

I don't know what my grandmother meant by being almost 10 years into the Kingdom and into the time of "Parousia", but it sounds like she had come to a place in her walk where she was learning to let go of shame and was begging my mom to do the same. In spite of my mom's restrictions, my grandmother tried hard to make an effort to stay within the boundaries my mom set so that they could still have some sort of a relationship. It was probably more of an effort than most mothers would have made to have a relationship with a child that they felt blamed them for everything going wrong in their life.

My mom never begged me to have a relationship with her even though at times, a lot of times, I blamed her for everything going wrong in my life. The hard truth of it is that after I was no longer living under my mom's roof, it was up to me to keep the relationship alive. Not that she didn't want a relationship with me, she did. Most days she didn't feel worthy enough to have a relationship with me, so she would not impose on me or bother me or force me to like her, let alone talk to her.

It was me. I was the one that begged her to have a relationship with me. I couldn't just stand by and not have a mother even if she was crazy and hurt my feelings. I was already a weirdo who grew up being pretty much raised as an adult. I didn't have a father, ever in the history of my friend-making years. Pretty much the fact that I had a living breathing person that fed me, clothed me, and put a roof over my head who was named "Mom" was the most normal thing I had in my life.

That wasn't all though. I quit thinking about how I got jipped and more about how she got jipped and realized that neither one of us asked to be born to the people that gave birth to us. That was God's decision for us, not ours. She grew angry about it and warned me not to do the same because anger would turn me bitter.

CHAPTER 4

One of the most gut wrenching entries was this one that I found written by my mom's five year old personality. I don't know if this came before or after the embarrassment of being undressed in front of total strangers, but I do know that she endured a situation that even grown adults have trouble navigating. I'll just let her tell you about it.

This is the journal entry titled 'The Witness,' written by my mom as an adult by her five-year-old self. It read:

"The Witness"

My little witness – or star witness he called me. John Stevens. They wanted me to feel special. Like maybe if I had told them I couldn't remember what they wanted me to remember then I would just be Helen and Bob's daughter.

But, since I could and I consented to witnessing on Uncle John's behalf I was now a special "little witness". Put stars and glitter around that

name.

My emotions were so cross-circuited I could not appreciate the honor. For one thing I wasn't sure I remembered, but I thought I did.

The end of the trial it was commented by all lawyers, supportive grown-ups "everyone had a different story." Did that mean I'd lied? Had I done something wrong? I thought I remembered Uncle John holding Mary while in the kitchen getting the other little girl a drink.

How could it be that there were so many different stories? How could people remember something so long ago? Did I lie? Would I go to hell? Surely my child-like understanding was in a traumatic state that day. But mostly because I'd embarrassed my Mom.

I rarely ever remember feeling much emotion around memories when I've embarrassed my Mom. Once done I couldn't undo it and all I wished is that I didn't exist. It would've been so much better for everyone if I hadn't been born. Cause to embarrass her was to make her wish she'd never been born.

And I'd embarrassed her of course. I always did. I couldn't wake up any day and think this will be a good day or a day I'll have fun. Cause I knew it was bound to happen. I'd embarrass her. But I think I never gave up. I always started out as a perfectionist whose ideal was to make it without one stumble to the top of the mountain. Yet more and more I found myself longing for my prison guards to be dead. And, of course, I'd probably go to hell for wishing that.

Anyway, back to my story. The "wishing they were dead fantasy" does tie in here to John Stevens. So maybe I better acknowledge it. My repetitive dream was that both my parents would die and I would be given to John and Martha Stevens to live with. I wasn't sure if anyone in the family would like me being there, but it didn't make any difference cause I would stay in my room and type on the typewriter they had. I would be typing all the time in my room. They wouldn't be bothered with me except at meals. Perhaps they could tolerate me just that much.

No, his daughters always seemed pretty snobbish to me. So my fantasy still couldn't even then allow that I would be happy. But I would endure. So hearing the favorable remarks from John

Stevens was good cause I wasn't sure he liked me either. Making my fantasy hard to really enjoy cause I didn't want to go to another place I wouldn't be liked really. They always liked everybody really so surely when my parents died, like in a car accident or something they'd adopt me.

Now logically that is hard to see why I thought that. I guess I assumed that if your parents died everyone would want to be nice to you and they'd ask you where you want to live. Guilt and shame were very real emotions that I felt. But were you accountable for dreams? Did you go to hell for dreams? I couldn't decide. I thought I had a 50/50 chance. But the 50% that said I'd probably be condemned to hell is what affected my emotions. And I lived everyday with guilt and shame.

So a little more about the trial. I was already accepting of my folly. But still the weight was heavier now. The guilt and shame I carried on my shoulders had been heavy enough, but now it was heavier. I'd have to convince myself I had remembered right. Then I wouldn't feel so bad. But I couldn't remember. I tried picturing what the lady across the street said hoping it would trigger my memory. I tried to hear what the girl said. It seemed to trigger a memory I didn't want to remember.

I remember we were sitting in the courtroom listening while she was giving her testimony. When she said Uncle John had put his hand on her crotch and told her not to tell anyone I looked up at John Stevens and shook my head "no". Thinking surely I could affirm that. Surely I would've remembered if he'd done that. Immediately after I did that the lawyer on the girl's side said, "If it please the court I'd like to ask that the audience in the courtroom to refrain from making any head gestures while witnesses are on the stand." Oops. I'd been bad again. But John Stevens just smiled at me so I guessed I wasn't going to hell.

So do you want to know what embarrassed my Mom? It was her fault. No wonder she wished she could die. I just realized Jean's (one of my mom's alters) thing about wishing she could die when trying to describe her emotions about why an event was bothering me so.

Diane, you embarrassed me so I could've just died.

I could've just dropped through the floor.

I could've dug a hole and covered it up over me.

I wished I was dead.

It was all I could do to keep from dying right there on the spot.

All of the above phrases I'm sure came out of my mother's mouth at one time or another. She used to have one about turning red as a beet. But I'd always wonder why was that so bad? Anyway, there was this rule. Don't use too many Kleenexs. Just take one and use it over and over until it won't work anymore. This is a pathetic story. I mean totally pathetic. And this part I've written before in my childhood history.

Here I was with snot running down my nose and a dilapidated Kleenex trying to wipe it and a really bad cold. And knowing that I looked really gross because her lawyer laid his head on the table and looked away. As if "I got to take time out to get sick".

Then he asked if someone else would take me a

box of Kleenex. But you're not supposed to blow your nose in public. So I had another problem. The lawyer was really hateful and intimidating. I mean I already felt like dirt, another of my Mom's expressions for embarrassing her, but he made me feel like shit. Only I didn't know that. I thought I was feeling really bad because I was bad. I had increased somehow drastically in my level of badness and now I was really bad. I'd swore on the Bible and said I remembered something I wasn't sure, but pretty sure I remembered.

My Mom wasn't supposed to talk about the story with me ahead of time, but she had and when they asked me if I'd talked it over with anyone I think I said yes. And that caused alot of trouble. No she hadn't, she told me later. Boy was I bad.

Or maybe I had said no, no one talked to me, but knew they had. Anyway, it seems like I remember Uncle John's lawyer coming to my defense saying something like we'd discussed the dates and time of day. It was like 6 months. We had moved at least once during that time.

Let's see. We lived in Southgate before the trial. I wonder if the trial thing might of held us up from moving a little. The day Uncle John was watching us kids I think we didn't have a house. I think that's what my parents were doing was house hunting and we were staying with Uncle John. He had two girls then and a wife, of course, and a big house in Yucaipa, California. He had just begun to be a successful contractor for these homes he was building and selling.

We stayed with Uncle John several times when we would move from Iowa to California. We'd come in on them in the middle of the night sometimes. Mom would be so embarrassed. Gosh. She just wished she was dead all the time. I remember one time we were there, but we stayed in the car for an hour or so. It must've been like 5:00 a.m. or something. No, she wanted us to stay in the car. We started to, but I had to use the bathroom. That's it. It was my fault for waking them up and everything.

You know I'd get in a lot of trouble for just normal body functions. Isn't that strange that people would want to put guilt and shame on you for something you couldn't control. I'll bet I got in trouble for making a mess when they gave me an enema. I'll bet I didn't get to the commode in time or something and really got gripped at. And I'll bet they used to make me feel

bad and responsible for doing things they were responsible for doing.

Diane Beadle – The Witness 4-15-1995

So there you have it as told by my mom.

I think it's important to know that I understand that people don't just wake up one day and decide to join a church that puts their children in harm. Somehow they got sucked in at a time when they were emotionally stressed and vulnerable.

I know I have been in the position, more than once, where something made sense at the time and later I realized I had been tricked or deceived. It's easy to want to put blame on someone else for making a child go through something like this even when I can't even fathom how they could, but they obviously were doing what they believed they were supposed to do to keep their family from going to hell and to survive life.

In addition to her journals, I also found some cassette tapes and booklets from John Robert Stevens. Wikipedia says that John Robert Stevens, "was an American pastor and cult leader who founded The Living Word Fellowship in the 1950s." I heard my mom and my grandmother refer to the Living Word Fellowship as "The Walk".

My opinion is that it probably grew into a cult, but at the beginning of the core of it was the belief that everyone should have a personal relationship with Jesus Christ. It can start off right, but if the focus on Jesus gets lost, then people also get lost. It's like they forget Who they are ministering for and their core rots as they distance themselves further from the truth.

My mom must have believed that what the news was saying was true because the day she heard it, she took every booklet and every cassette tape out of her house and put them in boxes in our carport saying that she would not have those things in her house. I don't know if you have had any experience with being in a cult or an over-the-top (for lack of a better word) type of religious organization, but the best way I can explain it is that it seems as though people get so caught up in becoming perfect in the eyes of the leaders, rather than what they believe is perfect in God's eyes.

She was so obsessed with being perfect in God's eyes. She had grown up under the teachings of John Robert Stevens and at one time she refused to believe that you can be perfect in God's eyes if you didn't become perfect in the way John Robert Stevens taught in his messages and teachings.

She must not have been totally convinced that all of his teachings were out of line, because I found a few booklets and tapes hidden away in a closet when I was packing up her things. People aren't just born evil, and even the most horrible people weren't always horrible.

Somewhere in their story there were moments, however small, where something good existed, even if it was buried under everything that came later. When I found those booklets, I just threw them away. I figured they were leftovers she missed when she was cleaning everything out. But she must have seen them when she moved. Right?

That was one of the things that happened all the time. She would get into a panic and in the peak of the emotional panic she would forget where she would lay something down or put something out of sight, inadvertently hiding things from herself. She would rarely call me just to talk because she didn't want to bother me. However, if she lost something, it was not unusual for me to get a phone call asking if I would come help her look.

That could be where I developed my supernatural finding abilities. I'm just kidding. There's really nothing supernatural about them, but when you have searched and found things so many times for someone else, I guess you develop an ability to find things and some people find that fascinating. Maybe it does border a little on being considered supernatural.

Of course, I'm just speculating now, but when my grandfather was removed from the role at the Mennonite church he'd been in his whole life, it was probably a little emotionally stressful for him. The church history of our family went back many, many, many years. I'm sure something about what John Stevens said must've made sense to him. From what I've been told in my research, some of my grandmother's siblings were considered "royalty" by the other members of the church. By the time my mom came along, I think most of my grandmother's brothers and sisters were in the church.

My grandfather would eventually leave, I'm pretty sure before my mom turned sixteen. As far as I know, he would never preach again. He and my grandmother divorced and almost immediately they both remarried. My grandfather would remain married until his death. My grandmother would divorce again and stay unmarried for her remaining years.

By the time my mom finally accepted that my grandmother could never undo the things that happened to her and decided to really forgive her for it, it was too late for my mom to tell her. My grandmother lived the last several years of her life with dementia and most likely would not have recognized my mom even if she had been able to make a trip to see her. My grandmother would continue to be an active member of the church John Robert Stevens had founded until she died in 2013, two weeks to the day after my mom passed away.

CHAPTER 5

A few months before my mom died, the pain from the cancer had gotten out of control. I took her to a respite facility to stay overnight so they could get it back under control. When I came back the next morning, her voice had changed. She sounded like her nose was stopped up and she was talking like a small child. I started to panic thinking everyone would find out now, but the doctor sensed my alarm at the sound of her voice and said that the medication he gave her more often than not makes people's voices change. I was relieved that he had given me an excuse before I had to think of one, but I was still skeptical about who I would find when I entered her room.

Closer to the end of her life, it seemed like most of her personalities had meshed together or went away. For the most part, if she kept her life simple and on schedule, she could manage her day to day without letting her anxiety drive her into a different personality. However, that day I still vividly remember the sound of her voice. There she was in all her glory, the five-year-old that had finally made her way to the place behind the eyes of my sixty-three year old mom.

My grandfather, Bob Roth, grew up as a Mennonite in Washington, Iowa. My great-grandfather was Mennonite and his father was Mennonite and his father before him was Mennonite. I was told by the family historian, my mom's sister, that the Mennonites were progressing forward as technology and machinery became available. That's when the Amish broke away from the Mennonites to protect their families from the world and preserve the old way of life.

I was fascinated by the Amish and so was my mom's sister. She also had a daughter, Tina, who was a little older than me. Most of my life she lived in California, Texas or Iowa. My mom took us to visit them in Houston, Texas, when I was around twelve and I think that was the last time I ever saw her. About seven years later she was in an accident and my aunt's heart seemed to forever be broken. The first details I heard about the accident, it seemed senseless and it was somebody's fault for letting it happen. Over the years, I would hear more details and it started to make sense that it was just that, an accident, but there wasn't anything I could say to convince her otherwise.

After Tina died, my aunt and I became close. We would talk on the phone for hours about new family discoveries she had made and I would tell her about any that I had made on my father's side. She had traced the family history back to when our ancestors were living overseas and owned castles and were Lords and Ladies.

Before Tina died, she showed us the family line of how David Lee Roth was our cousin. My mom forbade us to listen to Van Halen, but she usually wasn't home between the hours of eight in the morning and three in the afternoon so it was not unusual to hear "Jump" blaring from the album on the stereo console my step-dad brought with him when he moved in.

It seemed like my mom and my aunt's relationship was either close or strained. Most of the time you could wait a few days and it would all blow over. Of course, since they never saw each other, it was easier to get over, but it was also much easier to get away with pretending you're not mad.

My aunt lived in Iowa and my mom lived in Arkansas so all communication between them was by phone or letter. There were periods of time when my mom and my aunt would have disagreements and wouldn't talk for a while, but my aunt and I still talked during those times. Sometimes I felt like the buffer between them until they were able to resolve whatever their disagreement was.

During one of those periods that they were not communicating, my mom asked me not to tell her when I talked to my aunt because it brought up feelings she didn't want to deal with. I don't know why I thought it was a good idea at the time, but my aunt knew that I was running a business and needed a bookkeeper. She was in between jobs and needing to move. We decided that she should come work for me and live with me until she could find her own place.

At that time, my mom lived in Benton and I lived in Malvern, about 30 miles apart. It wasn't like they would run into each other at Walmart. My mom rarely came to my house unless it was the holidays and since it was early in the year, I just decided I would figure out later what to do when it came time for all that.

Looking back now, it looks like I didn't care about my mom's feelings. I did, but I really thought I could get away with my mom not finding out my aunt was even there. I got what I needed, my aunt got what she needed and when my mom found out, I would deal with it then. I'll admit my priorities were definitely out of whack. At that time, I cared more about my business succeeding and reconciled all the pros and cons to mean that my aunt moving in with me would be a good thing.

The minute she pulled up to my house in Arkansas after leaving Iowa, she asked me to call my mom and let her know she was there. I knew right then I had made a mistake. Fortunately, that bad decision didn't last forever. Unfortunately, during that time my business failed and my whole life fell apart.

When I refused to do anything to stop the chaos in my life that was growing more and more out of control, my aunt got mad and left.

While my aunt was living with me, she did share her knowledge of the ancestry of our family. However, by the time she died, she had disowned the entire family, converted to the Mormon faith and gave them our family history. She told me that my grandfather was forbidden to go to war and because he did it anyway, they booted him out of the family.

Thanks to Ancestry, I found his discharge papers and found out that he was classified as a 1-A-O conscientious objector since he opposed serving in the military because of his religious beliefs. It was confirmed by my grandfather's family when I attended my first ever Roth family reunion in 2021, that my grandfather and his brother were both conscientious objectors. My grandfather served in the Army at the 130th Station Hospital in Heidelberg, Germany during WWII.

In my mind the story about being banished from the family was pretty believable because not only did he join the Army, but he obviously was not a Mennonite anymore. At the reunion, his family told me that they were removed from the church roll because they enlisted in the service.

After my grandfather left the military service, he came back to Iowa and married my grandmother. The only details I know are from very limited knowledge and from public records, so I have no idea how or why they met, what he liked about her, or what she liked about him.

I don't know what she dreamed the perfect family looked like. I'll just have to skip over that part.

What I do know is that my grandfather began going to my grandmother's church and after he became friends with John Stevens, he became a preacher. He and my grandmother would have revivals in city parks. My grandmother would play the guitar and my mom and my aunt, who were then both under the age of five or six, would sing along with her. My grandfather would preach.

I have no idea how many times they stopped along the way or how long they stayed in one place, but somehow they made their way from Iowa to Los Angeles, California.

At one of these revivals, my mom remembered singing a hymn or some song with my aunt while my grandmother played the guitar. After they were finished with the song, she went skipping through the park when a man stopped her.

He squatted down to her level so he could look her in the eyes and then started screaming at her. Near the end of her life my mom desperately tried to remember the words he was saying.

She would close her eyes and tell me she could still see how red his face was and feel the spit flying out of his mouth onto her face while he was screaming at her, but she could not remember what it was he was saying. She opened her eyes.

"I think I would like to go color now."

It was Margaret again. By this time, I had talked to Margaret several times and was starting to actually like her. Margaret was about five years old and sounded as though her nose was stopped up and very much like a five-year-old that was in that learning stage between baby talk and big kid talk.

No matter how much assurance I gave my mom that she was safe and the red-faced man wasn't there, Margaret refused to let her remember what it was he told her. I would leave her alone with her color books and crayons.

Several more times over the course of a few weeks, we would try again for my mom to remember what it was that Margaret was hiding from her so well. My mom would think back, this particular time, keeping her eyes open and looking at me hoping that would help her focus.

"I do remember something. The sun was shining. It was warm and I had a flowy dress on. I could spin around and my dress would fly up around me. My mother gave me money to go buy some gum. I was going to go buy some gum. Then this man stopped me. He was an old man. He was screaming. What was he saying? What did I do that was so bad?"

I held my breath while I looked in her eyes hoping she would stay with me long enough to remember what he said. Then I saw her eyes shift and her face went blank.

"Do you know the song Jesus loves me?"

It was Margaret again. Whatever it was, Margaret made sure that it was a secret that would go with her when she took Jesus by the hand and flew away.

On a very yellowed piece of typing paper, I found the journal entry below. The page was brittle around the edges like it had been tucked away for years. I could almost hear the keys of her typewriter hitting the ribbon with each letter landing with a firm little thud.

My memory for today was that of a little girl about four years old (it was me). I remember walking through a crowd of people who had just finished watching me sing. There was a park in the center of Wayland and an open air band stand. It was there I sang a song "My Mommy told me something a little girl should know it was all about the devil and how I learned to hate him soo. When ever he came in a room he filled it up with gloom (not sure what comes next). Then I just open ... and let the sunshine in. Just let the sunshine in face him with a grin. Frowners always lose and smilers always win. Just let the sunshine in face him with a grin open up your heart and let the sunshine in.

Nice little song. Much to the detriment of my little inner child. She now believes smiling and frowning are all important stuff. I told her it wasn't of course but she's not convinced. Also she goes back from the store, and tells her Mommy something or tries to tell her something. We can't seem to remember what it was that was upsetting her. She remembers telling people about getting to buy some gum. Their response to her made

her feel uncomfortable. I believe her mommy is embarrassed by something she's done. She doesn't seem to know what it is but she's sure she shouldn't have done it. And so that is about it. I'm not sure I used my time wisely. I thought I needed to cry. I do but how when all is under lock and key.

I'm not sure that you can even describe with enough detail what it's like talking to a five-year-old version of your mother for you to truly realize what was happening to me and her at the time. The first time I met Margaret, my mom was at a respite facility talking to the doctor like a five-year-old. She asked the doctor if she could have a sucker because she had been good. I just laughed and said, "ya'll must have given her some good drugs!"

It was that very moment that I made the decision to take her home with me. When I told her she was going to come live with me, her five-year-old self was much more excited than I knew her sixty-three year old self would be if she knew what was going on. The doctor told me that he wanted to keep her one more day. My mind couldn't process at the time all the things that could go wrong with her staying another night, so I didn't fight it. I had to get home and get my house ready for my mom and my younger sister to move in.

She had acted out before by looking like a completely different person, and not just a different personality. She changed her hairstyle, wore clothing she wouldn't normally wear and had an unfamiliar accent in her speech. It wasn't something that would happen on a normal basis and happened only twice that I could vividly recall, but if I had to be honest about what happened, I would say that she did it to embarrass me. She had stopped by my house unannounced and hair was up in some sort of weird bun and she tried to talk with a thick southern accent as opposed to her undeniable west coast way that she talked.

Fortunately, when I went back to the facility to pick her up, she was back to being herself. When we initially found out that she had about a year left, we started discussing what life would look like towards the end. She agreed that when I said it was time to come live with me, that she wouldn't argue, she would just go and believe it was the way it needed to be. I broke the news to her that it was time for her to come home with me. She let out a long sigh and said, "Okay."

One morning, closer to the end of her time with me, she had just woken up. Her voice was drastically different like the voice of a very small child.

"I'm really scared. I can't find my baby. I need my baby."

I was so freaking mad. I wanted to scream. One of those screams you can let out when you're by yourself because you've lost just about every smidge of sanity you have because the one thing that's been going right just got snatched away from you as you were reaching out to shield it from being taken because you had gotten so used to it being that way. That kind of scream. If you've never screamed like that, you should try it. At this moment, I could only scream like that inside because it was my mom. It wasn't her fault, but the moments she was awake when I got to talk to the sixty-three-year-old "her" were getting shorter, fewer and farther between. She asked me not to tell anyone about her multiple personality disorder until after she was gone, but she had never acted so convincingly young. The doctor had prescribed stronger pain medication, so it would also be easy to say the medication was causing hallucinations.

In the past I could tell her what year it was, how old I was, or show her pictures of her grandchildren to kind of remind her who she was and where she was in case she seemed confused, but this time nothing was working. So, I told her that all of her babies were grown. My eyes got big as her face got bright red.

"I don't have babies! I need my baby doll!"

She had told me once that some of her personalities had items of their own. I assumed Margaret had crayons and coloring books. Another had paper dolls and a crossword puzzle book. She said nothing about a baby doll, but I set off to her house, which was 30 minutes away, in search of a baby doll. After coming up empty handed, I ended up compromising on borrowing a baby doll. Once I got back home with the baby doll in tow, she was asleep again.

The next time she woke up, she was hallucinating again, talking about the stairs being on fire and she couldn't climb up to get to the door to get out and about the baby doll. She screamed about the baby doll. I tried to give her the doll. She pushed it away.

I was terrified. I don't consider myself an extremely skeptical person, but I do not want to ever be considered naive. If there was something tormenting her soul before she died, I couldn't just sit there and not do anything so I called her pastor.

She quieted down and it was over. Her last few days after that would be more peaceful. I played worship music in her room on repeat until she took her last breath. *The Voice of Truth* and the voices of all her children laughing. It was the last thing she heard here on earth.

Between the drugs and the emotional distress of dying and the broken pieces of her and the path of trauma that laid behind her suddenly started making more and more sense.

CHAPTER 6

This journal entry was one she wrote not long before she moved from Little Rock to Benton, Arkansas. Back when she was still with my step-dad. Back before she tried to figure out how many personalities she had. Back when I thought her life would have been so much simpler if she had been oblivious to her mental illness.

My step-dad told me once that "she should've never taken the lid off that can of worms". I know she wanted to know what was wrong with her, but sometimes I wonder how different life would have been if she had never been told that she had multiple personality disorder.

5:00 a.m.I feel angry cause I can not sleep. I want to sleep. I am tired. I will be tired later and now I can't sleep. I feel angry because when I don't sleep well I am tired all day. I haven't been able to work well. I haven't been able to have fun. I am too tired. Robert woke me up because I was howling in my sleep. From then on I haven't slept well. Finally, I got up. I wrote about the dream in dreams book. I feel out of sorts, grump. Things are not going well. This personality that

I am right now I think is a grumpy one. Just grouchy and grumpy. The last one I recognized was Linda. She ended Friday though and grumpy started Saturday. I wish I knew why I am so grumpy. Mom

Once she was given the diagnosis of multiple personality disorder, it seemed like her life became more complicated. In order for her to have some kind of peace in her life, she became consumed with trying to make all of her personalities happy. I guess maybe she thought personalities like "grumpy" would be less grumpy and make her life easier if she could figure out what it was they needed to be happy, but it also meant having to find out why they were grumpy in the first place. When you figure out you have fifty-three personalities to try to make get along, it can get a little overwhelming.

My grandmother on my mom's side, Helen, said something about how she shouldn't disturb the roots. My grandmother on my dad's side, Esther, told me not to disturb the skeletons in the closet.

Knowing what I know now about my past and generational curses, it just made my life make more sense. I didn't want to know about the past to try to change the past. I only wanted to know to try to make it make sense.

I learned so much of what I know now from experiencing life with her the way I did. I also learned that hearing about the past from other perspectives makes the past make better sense. For myself, it made sense that digging up those roots and examining those skeletons would make room for better memories.

A little over a year had passed since I had run the 62 mile race that was going to be the last race of my running career, when I decided to run a much shorter, 12-and-a-half-mile race in Benton, Arkansas. I looked at the course map before I ran it, but I didn't really study it. It started and ended at the new Boys and Girls Club.

The morning of the race it was raining and it seemed like the temperatures had all the sudden dropped, which was fine. It was good running weather except for the rain. Once we started, I decided the more running and the less walking I did, the faster I would finish and be able to get into dry clothes so my goal then was to just keep a pace I could maintain to run the whole race without walking.

As I started running my thoughts took over, as they usually did, and I thought about how most of my life I've been running, not quite in the literal sense of being a runner, but running from my past, running from my problems, running from life, running from my mom and the lingering memories.

It seemed like if I wasn't running from my life, I was at least planning an escape route just in case. There weren't really too many times in my life that I could think of where I was content with just being where I was, until that moment. At that moment I felt like I could finally quit running from my life. I finally felt like I could embrace my life and just run, in the literal sense.

After a couple miles in, the course took a turn and I started down a short hill. I could see the long uphill in front of me and it hit me that I was running on the same road I had driven up hundreds of times. We were headed right to my mom's old house. The house she moved into when she and my step-dad separated. The house I dreaded her moving into because she was going to live too close.

Back around 1995, I moved to Benton from Little Rock. I was working for an attorney as a "do it yourself" paralegal. I knew nothing about being a paralegal, but I did know I needed a divorce and I knew how to type. After a few phone calls, I found an attorney that was in need of a secretary and took me up on my offer to trade out typing for divorce representation. I must have been decent at what I did because he kept me working full-time until I decided it was time to go somewhere else.

Right before that, I was waiting tables at Chili's and trying my best to get good grades at a community college studying graphic design. It was hard to make ends meet on a waitress salary and I was too embarrassed to go ask for help from anyone, much less government assistance. I ditched school with only two months left to finish. I thought I was doing the same thing everyone else did that needed to better themselves, but like with most things in my life, I couldn't afford it. My kids had to eat. It's been that way all my life. Every time I thought I could afford something, I realized I could at the moment, but I never could afford to keep it.

As I reached the top of the hill, the course turned and there it was. I thought to myself, just don't look at it, but it was hard to miss. Someone had painted it a dark green with white trim. It was so much different than the bright white house it used to be. It sat on the corner directly in front of the water stop for the race. You couldn't miss it. It was right there just glaring at me.

I couldn't see past my own problems back then, before she moved into this house, to realize what was going on in her life. She and my step-dad were on the verge of separating. My little brother was seventeen and doing what most other seventeen year old boys were doing back then, except for being reproductive.

It was strange to me, because he had a girlfriend. He babysat for me in exchange for rides to go see her. We were still just as close as we'd always been, even though I'd already moved out, so I knew it wasn't because he couldn't. It was because of his faith in God that he wanted to wait. I was proud of him for that. It was a decision that had been too hard for me to make.

I turned the corner and a flood of emotion came over me. All of the sudden I had a flash of memories of all the time I had spent in that house. The times I spent there during the holidays, the times we had birthday celebrations that were never for me, the times I just needed to lay on her couch, the times she prayed for me, the times she told me everything was going to be okay and the times I knew everything would be okay.

Tears started drizzling down my cheeks. I couldn't stop them. All I wanted to do at that moment was to stop running and wait for her to come back home. Fortunately, it was raining so I don't think anyone noticed the tears. About the time I headed for the driveway, I literally almost ran over a running friend who had taken the early start and was coming towards me. It startled me enough to remind me that I was out here running a race.

And then I did what I always do, I made a U-turn on Memory Lane and came back to reality. There would be time to grieve my loss later. Right then, I just needed to run my race. For the rest of the race I concentrated on running and trying to catch up with my running friend.

Since then I went back and revisited Memory Lane and let myself think about that house. When my mom first moved there, she was worried about having enough money to pay the rent. She was always worried about having enough money, but somehow she always seemed to have enough. She told me once that she had the faith to eat vegetables and she thought I must have the faith to eat meat because I spent my money on things that she couldn't justify for herself.

One of the things I learned from her when she was living in that house was that there was always a way to make a few dollars here and there to have what you needed. Ebay had just become popular and I showed her how to use it to make some extra money. Having a personality that liked to collect things must have helped her because she loved going to yard sales and finding things she could sell on Ebay. Also, there were several families she cleaned house for that would clean out their closets and leave nice things for her to have. She would take the treasures home and put it on Ebay to sell. It wasn't long before she had a pretty good little side hustle going and she made decent money at it.

When she was setting up her account on Ebay, she needed to come up with a name for her side business. I can't remember all of the names she had thought of, but she settled on *The Gleaning Heiress*. At the time I thought it was a dumb name, but then she explained that gleaning in the Bible was when poorer people went and harvested grain, or other crops, that were purposely left by the owners for them to come and get.

The heiress part was because she was an heiress of Jesus. She always identified herself as being poor and she belonged to Jesus, so it fit her uniqueness perfectly.

Going to yard sales and collecting things to sell not only gave her extra money, it was also something my sister and I enjoyed doing with her. I thought she had finally figured out a way to appease the personality that wanted to collect things, the personality that worried about money, the personality that wanted to have fun, the personality that wanted to spend time with her girls and even the personality that was so grumpy.

When I was cleaning out her house after she died, she had more things that were tagged and ready to sell than she had nice things for herself.

We spent a lot of the holidays at this house. Holidays with my mom were weird, especially Christmas, but Thanksgiving was special for me and her. It was the one holiday we both enjoyed and agreed on how it should be celebrated. She tried so hard to make it good for everyone, but sometimes her cooking was never good no matter how hard she tried.

She would get anxious in the middle of cooking and start having doubts about how her family felt about her and then from there ingredients would get left out or too much put in, food would get left in the oven too long and burn, but she always tried so hard.

The one thing you could count on was her having out the video camera. She loved making family videos. She told me once that she didn't get to see her boys that often and being able to watch the videos later kept her from missing them so much. It also let her see if there was anything she missed if she switched personalities. After dinner she liked to play board games. Of course not everyone wanted to play, but I wish I would have insisted that they do it anyway. You never really knew what to expect as far as the food went, but once the food was ready and everyone started showing up she was always so happy we were all there.

When she started resorting to ordering the Thanksgiving meal from one of the local restaurants, I decided it was time for me to start cooking Thanksgiving dinner. We started having Thanksgiving at my house and she would come, but I knew she was never as comfortable as she was when we had it at her house. Of course, the way I was living my life had to be acceptable to her or she wouldn't come. If I was living with someone that I wasn't married to, she wouldn't come to my house.

My life always seemed to be hard. It didn't matter if I knew what I was doing was right or wrong. I just did what I thought was best for all involved with what short-term consequences I could live with. There were times when I felt like even just getting from one day to the next was a struggle. I couldn't take into consideration the long-term consequences of it all because the only thing I knew to do was to try to make everyone around me happy day to day.

It seems to me that looking back, at one point in my life I thought my purpose was to be a perfect little real life doll for my mom. I don't even know where I got that idea because my mom always told me to be what Jesus told me to be. Jesus never told me to be my idea or anyone else's idea of the perfect little real life doll.

The idea might have been planted from looking at photo albums with my grandparents. We only saw them every other year or so and when they would come over, out would come the pictures.

One of them would point to a picture of younger, less troubled me, and say, "*oh, you look like a real life doll.*"

Of course, it was most always followed with, "*but, why aren't you smiling.*"

From there things would usually take an awkward turn and I'd do what I did best and make people uncomfortable and they would let me leave and go be alone with my thoughts.

One Thanksgiving my grandmother, Helen, was there and my mom had either just started dating or had just married my step-dad. I had a horrible case of snot residing in every orifice I had.

At around eleven years old, prior to my smoking days, sometimes in order for me to resume breathing, it sounded like I was hacking up a lung and I would expel what would come up by spitting it out. I did it in a tissue, but my grandmother was mortified.

She grabbed me by the arm, marched me down the hallway into the master bedroom and shoved me through the door of the master bathroom and told me to stay there.

It wasn't bad enough that I was pretty sure I was not supposed to be in the master bathroom, mostly because I knew I was most definitely not allowed to be in the master bedroom, but she then proceeded to scold me for being an embarrassment to my mother.

Things like this happened to me all the time. People who barely knew me, people who floated in and out of my life for short seasons, acted like they had the authority to name who I was. And I let them. They were the adults, and I assumed they must be seeing something true. It took me more than forty years to understand how far off they were.

They didn't know me. They didn't even know themselves well enough to speak truth over anyone else. They were just trying to keep the peace, to hold everything together with whatever thin thread they had. If everyone looked happy, they could pretend they were, too. And somewhere in all of that, I can see now how much fear was running the show. Fear dressed up as authority, fear disguised as concern, fear pretending to be wisdom.

Looking back, I can see the grace in it too. They were doing the best they knew how, even if it wasn't good. They didn't know what they were doing. But God did. And He's the one who kept the truth intact until I was finally ready to see it.

Even before I knew she was dying, I wanted my brothers to never regret the time they spent with my mom. I wanted the time my daughters remember having with my mom to be time spent with a grandmother that seemed a little eccentric, but somewhat normal, but most of all loved them. I wanted my mom to feel loved and accepted. I just wanted to fix it.

In spite of that, it seemed like my brothers enjoyed making the holidays a game of *how long will mom stay this time*. I begged them to please play by "mom's rules" until she left which meant don't cuss, don't talk about politics and don't drink.

After dinner was over and we were sitting around talking, she would be so afraid of what she called "changing personalities", that the minute someone would start talking a little too raunchy or loud for her taste or pop open a beer, she would all the sudden stand up and say

"*I'm leaving now. Goodbye.*" and then walk out the door.

That's how it was. Every. Single. Time.

To me it seemed like my brothers played on taunting my mom and joked that if she stayed she would turn into a raging monster growing horns out of her head. It was like their annual holiday cheer in every sense of the word.

If they would have seen the raging monster I had seen her be not long before, I don't know that they would have pushed her to her limits every time, but she knew where her limit was and she never let them get that far. When they pushed that safety boundary line so taut that the string was about to break, she would just stand up and said, "*Goodbye*" and off she would go before she turned into that monster that spewed venom, righteous or not, over anyone in her path.

It most definitely is changing personalities. It's changing into a cussing, screaming, raging lion from a humble, meek, wounded sheep that's been attacked by a lion too many times. It used to make me so angry that they would do that to her, but she would just laugh and tell me not to worry about it.

The exit we had rehearsed over and over had worked and no one got hurt. Except for me. I knew it then and I know it now, but for the small price of me just letting it go and letting them have their fun, she got as much of a "*normal*" Thanksgiving as she could have for where her circumstances in life had brought her.

The food was better because we cooked and she didn't, but now I realize it wasn't the food that was so important. I never thought I would miss it, but I really miss her dressing that tastes like cardboard because that means she would be there too, but then again, were she still living, I wouldn't have learned everything I know now.

CHAPTER 7

So many memories are stashed away inside me, and the very first ones start when I was around three years old. We lived in England, Arkansas, where most of my dad's brothers and sisters lived, along with my grandmother.

My dad's history was already marked by tragedy before I was born. In 1943, when he was almost three years old, his five-year-old sister was run over and killed by an automobile. My grandmother used to say that was back when I was just a "twinkle in my daddy's eye," so I can only imagine what his own childhood memories must have been like.

My grandmother never learned to drive and never owned a vehicle, but all of my uncles and my dad drove muscle cars and trucks. When my dad wasn't performing music, he and my uncle owned and ran Burkett Brothers Mechanic Shop. As hard as I've tried to outrun the family line of business, I, too, have found myself in the automotive industry at one time or another. It seems oil and grease are in the bloodline.

My mom gave birth to me when she was twenty-two, barely fifteen months after my older brother was born. My dad would have been about thirty-one. Less than ten years later, he would pass away from lung cancer and cirrhosis of the liver, consequences of heavy smoking and drinking. I'm not sure at what point he became an alcoholic, but I'm guessing it started long before he turned thirty for it to kill him at barely forty.

If you come from my family, there's just not a lot of time between being a kid and being an independent adult. Ask me how I know.

My mom worked as a waitress at a cafe at the edge of town. As an adult, I've driven by the building several times. I can't remember if it's still a cafe, but I always look at the parking lot and remember the day my dad and his buddies pulled a flatbed trailer in there to use as a stage.

My mom was so happy that day. She was married to the man she must have always wished for, the man all the other girls wished they could have. It sounds like the perfect life, but the problem was that my dad granted one too many girls their wishes. My mom either didn't know or didn't care that his other girlfriends were there that day. I just know she was happy. I could feel it. There was enough excitement in the air to make her forget, even if she did know.

She told me they met around 1969. She was working as a waitress at a diner near Redlands, California. One day, her ears perked up when she heard my dad singing on the radio. The DJ announced that "The Sundowners" were going to be performing in Bakersfield.

When she told me this story, she conveniently left out the venue. It wasn't until I was much older, and learned about the real life of country music singers, that I realized the performance was at a bar. She wouldn't tell me that because she didn't want to put him in a "poor light." To her, "poor light" was anything associated with bars and drinking.

I tried so many times to get her to tell me which bar it was, but I was unsuccessful. It was unnecessary trauma I brought on myself, I wouldn't just let it go. I've screamed some pretty mean things at her in my mind over the years. I didn't know she was screaming right back at me until I started reading her journals. She couldn't see the anger on my face, and I never could see it on hers.

The important part of the story is that when she saw him in Bakersfield that night, she told herself, *I'm going to marry that man.* The rest is history. Although it is short, it is one of my favorite love stories simply because it's one of the few she ever told me about my dad.

Because she shared so little, I realize now that I was desperate for my dad to be someone greater than who he was. If I never really knew him, I could make him be whoever I wanted. With the few details I had, I could build him up in my mind to be a better dad than anyone else's. It used to be important to me to tell my friends that he was a hero, because that was the only way to override the first-hand knowledge I actually had.

Once I quit being so angry with my mom for not sharing her memories, I was able to recover some actual good memories of my own. I finally see that Memory Lane isn't just one big, bad road. There are good stops along the way, too.

Like the time my dad got me my very own horse.

I got to ride her every chance I had. No one could convince five-year-old me that I wasn't strong enough to throw a saddle on her, let alone tighten the belly strap. My parents must have been relieved when I finally got tired of asking for help and learned to ride bareback.

I would climb up on the gate of the fence, just like I had seen my dad do. When my horse came close, I would grab her mane and throw my leg over her back. Our pasture was fenced, so there was no danger of her running off with me. My mom would just tell me to go play outside, so when I wasn't riding, I was exploring the woods with my other friends: the barn animals.

My friends were my horse, a cat with twelve kittens, the pigs, and the chickens.

Well, the chickens were my friends until I went into their coop and got attacked. Coincidence or not, soon after that attack, my grandfather chopped off their heads. I watched the headless bodies jump and run around the yard. So when people say someone is "running around like a chicken with their head cut off," I don't just imagine it. I know exactly what that looks like.

The real reason he killed them was likely because they were too much for my mom to take care of by herself, but at least we had plenty of food for a while.

Then the good stops on Memory Lane get further apart and the stops like the loss of the horse hit harder.

One morning, I woke up and looked out the window. My horse was gone. Barefooted and in my nightgown, I ran outside to where my dad was standing. I was bawling my eyes out. He picked me up and told me that our stallion had broken the fence and my horse had escaped. He said he was really sorry.

It made no sense to me why only *my* horse had escaped while the stallion was still there, but he said that's what happened, and I believed him.

It wasn't long after that I overheard my mom telling someone that my dad had traded my horse for a new drum set. It was obvious she wasn't happy about it. Life for us started changing pretty fast after that.

Because my dad was already gone so much, I never really knew when my parents separated. Every now and then he would come pick us up and take us to his girlfriend's house, but sometimes he would still stay at our house, too. My young childish self didn't know there was anything wrong with that arrangement. All I knew was that nobody ever told me I couldn't love them both. Actually, nobody said much of anything to me. Most likely because I didn't have much to say to them.

Being in the front seat at seven years old feels like being on stage when you've spent your whole life trying to blend into the wallpaper. There I was, tucked into the upholstery of a car traveling from Texas back to Little Rock, sitting right next to the man himself. If it had to do with music or God, it had my attention and this man was our worship pastor.

By then, the silence wasn't just a habit, it was my armor. I had been "stoic" since before I had the vocabulary to describe it. I didn't say much, but I was a world-class observer.

As we crossed the line back into Arkansas, we passed a sign for a town called Lamar. My brain, which was always firing a million miles a minute behind my shut mouth, immediately clicked. *Lamar.* I looked at the man in the driver's seat, then back at the sign, and I was absolutely certain that this man was so important he had an entire town named after him. It was a classic "kid logic" moment, the kind I look back on now and just have to laugh at.

I sat there desperately wanting him to look at the silent, stoic girl next to him and decide to keep me. I wanted him to adopt me, to pluck me out of the bad TV show I was living in and rewrite the script. I was already looking for a way out before I even knew what I was running from.

Then I get whisked back into real life. My life. Where the monsters lived that I had to fight. Through the eyes of a kid, peeking out from behind the shadows, I started noticing other people's lives looked way different than mine.

It was Halloween. My dad and his girlfriend took me trick-or-treating dressed up as a bunny rabbit. She painted my nose pink with her lipstick and drew whiskers on my cheeks with her eyeliner.

I went up to a house, and as I turned to leave, the man at the door spoke up.

"*Hang on a second. I've got something special for you.*"

He came back with an apple.

I walked down the steps, and I could hear the skepticism in my dad's voice when he asked to see what the man had given me.

I held up the apple.

He took it out of my hand, looked it over, and I saw his face turn blood red. He stormed up the steps, grabbed the man by his collar, and hit him square in the face with my apple.

I couldn't keep from crying. A lot. Still to this day I can feel the knot that started to develop in my throat before the flood of tears came.

My dad and his girlfriend checked every single piece of candy before they would let me have it. They let me eat as many as I wanted just to get me to stop sobbing.

Not long after that car ride, my dad must have been so tormented with his thoughts, it reached the breaking point of our little family unit.

I walked through the double doors of the church into the sanctuary. Everyone was already on their knees with their heads down on the pews, praying.

There was a sinking feeling in my gut, like something really bad must have happened. My mom scooted me into one of the rows and told me to crawl under the pew.

I didn't know what was going on that day. It wasn't until years later, after my mom had died, that a lady from the church told me the truth: My dad had gotten drunk and told my mom that if she went to church, he was going to go down there and shoot the pastor.

I know my dad can sound like a terrifying figure to someone hearing about him for the first time. A violent, raging alcoholic most of the time I remember him. Someone unpredictable, someone who could turn a room into a battlefield without ever raising a weapon. But that's not the only version of him I carry. The memories I have are all I have, and they don't separate into tidy piles. They come as one whole thing. Fear woven into love, danger woven into tenderness, brokenness woven into the few moments where he tried.

I saw the man who scared me, yes. But I also saw the man who loved me in the only ways he knew how. The man shaped by wounds he never healed from, by a childhood that taught him survival but not peace. His story didn't start with the violence I remember; it started with his own pain, handed down long before I was born.

And I haven't always carried those memories well. For years, they were too heavy, too tangled, too confusing to hold without either dropping them or pretending they didn't exist. My relationship with Jesus changed that. Not by erasing the past, but by giving me a place to set the weight down and let Him sort through what I couldn't. He taught me that truth and grace can sit in the same room without fighting. He taught me that I don't have to choose between honesty and compassion.

So when I say this is the only way I know how to carry him, I mean it. I carry him the way God has taught me to carry anything that's both beautiful and broken. I carry them with truth, with honesty, and with a grace that doesn't excuse anything, but also doesn't erase the parts that were real. I can't pretend he was all good. I can't pretend he was all bad. I carry him as both, because that's the truth.

And somehow, even in the mess of it, I trust that God sees the whole story, his, mine, all of it, and holds what I can't. Which is good, because the next part of this story isn't exactly light reading. If you need to stretch, take a sip of water, or emotionally brace yourself, now's your moment.

The dad I knew was a country music singer and a truck driver. There was no other man in the world that could make my eyes light up the way he did. Despite everything he did to my mom, she never once let me know if she hated him or not and when she allowed him to see us, it felt like Christmas morning and not just because he always brought us presents.

Speaking of Christmas, that was the one thing my mom and dad fought about almost as much as the drinking.

I have never truly understood why my mom didn't like Christmas, but in one of her journal entries, she wrote about a memory from when she was young. Her mother took her to California right before the holidays and told her not to tell her dad she wasn't coming back after that visit. My mom felt like she had betrayed her dad by keeping that secret, even though she was just a child. My best guess is that her contempt for the holiday started there, tangled up with that early heartbreak. And probably mixed with a handful of other moments where her feelings got bruised, twisted around, and left sitting in the dark without anyone helping her sort them out.

Christmas of 1977, we lived in a run-down single-wide trailer in Mabelvale, Arkansas. My mom was working as a waitress at a cafe in a hotel off the interstate. We were poorer than dirt, though my brother and I didn't know it. My mom said we weren't having a Christmas tree that year. We assumed she couldn't afford one. I know now that she just didn't *want* one.

One morning before she got home from work, my brother and I took her good serrated knife and marched out to a row of pine trees between our house and my dad's cousin's house next door.

We sawed through the trunk of a tree that was taller than we were, covering ourselves in sticky sap and pine needles. We dragged it into the house and leaned it against the wall because we didn't have a stand.

When my mom came home, she was furious that we had ruined her knife. But then, looking at our faces, something shifted. She decided it was okay. She helped us stand it up and decorate it.

On Christmas Day, my dad walked in the door after being gone for weeks. His arms were full of presents.

My mom took one look at them and a fight broke out. She refused to let him give us the gifts unless he took the labels off and wrote that they were from him. She yanked a present out of his hand and threw it on the floor. I saw my name on it. The tag said "From Santa."

My dad yelled, "There's not a damn thing wrong with letting these kids believe in Santa! For God's sake, they ain't got much as it is, just let them have this!"

I begged her to let us open them. I promised her we knew they were really from him. Eventually, she relented. I got a silver necklace with a heart pendant. My mom told him it was dumb to get me something I was just going to lose.

I promised I wouldn't lose it. Of course, I did eventually, but I still remember exactly what it looked like. To me, that heart contained all my daddy's love. I knew he had fought for me to have it.

Now, back to that Sunday afternoon at the church, the day he threatened our family with being on the six o'clock news.

My dad was home off the road, and he was drunk. My brother and I had been outside playing. One of us opened the door to go inside, and the scene froze us in place.

There sat my mom in the living room, tied up in a chair.

My dad was holding a gun to her head.

I try to think back to what must have been going through my mind, but all I can remember is my mom's voice. She looked at us and said, "It's okay. We are playing Cowboys and Indians. Just go back outside."

There's no doubt in my mind that it had to be the Holy Spirit doing the talking through her. Whoever it was made sure we felt safe.

My dad put the gun down on the coffee table and untied her.

I crawled up in his lap.

The threat must have still been there, but the rage had subsided for the moment. I asked my mom about that day a few years before she died. She couldn't, or maybe she just didn't want to, recall anything more than bits and pieces.

She did reveal that the incident with the gun was the last straw. That evening, we came home from church, and she started packing a suitcase.

In the middle of the night, she woke us up, put us in the car, and drove hours away to Hamburg, Arkansas. We stayed with people she said were from the church. My only vivid memory of that time is sitting on a porch swing, waiting for her to come back from her shift at Shoney's Big Boy.

And waiting for life to start over again.

CHAPTER 8

One of the hardest journal entries for me to read and process was this one my mom wrote:

> **How do I work through this issue? I guess I realize. Yes. I did the wrong thing. I did a thing that my children might never be able to forgive me for.**
>
> **I did it and I am sorry. I can not believe I would do something that would cause so much pain, emotional pain, to my children. Yet, I better believe it.**
>
> **I did it and the pain of that last memory will forever be etched in their minds and mine.**

The issue she is talking about happened in January or February of 1982. I was 9 years old. We stayed in Hamburg for about a month the best I can recall. When we got back to Mabelvale, my mom was more serious than ever about starting over.

My dad must've been serious about starting over too. Somewhere in between 1980 and 1982, he moved to Arlington, Texas and married a lady named Linn.

Trying to figure out how old I might have been at the time a certain incident happened based on my younger self's point of view usually takes some analytical effort, but the day she's talking about, I know so well I can pinpoint the date. As a matter of fact, that is the day I use as a reference point for where I was mentally, spiritually and physically at the age of just prior to 10 years old because it all comes back so vividly clear.

If my visits with my dad were limited to phone calls on purpose, I didn't know it and still don't know for sure that they were. It wasn't unusual to talk to him on the phone and then see him the next day. He had traveled for all his jobs as long as I had known him. The last few times I had seen him the police were involved, but my mom always told us that he would be back after a while to get us when he was feeling better.

That day I knew it had been longer than usual since I had seen him. It had gotten really bad the last time, but I can still feel the longing of wanting to know where he was and when he was going to come get me.

I knew that people had better houses, better clothes and better things than we did, but at that time of my life, I didn't care what they had. I had what I had and it was fine. There wasn't any idea in my head that I should compare my own life to someone else's who had more or less than me. I knew our lifestyles were different, but I thought I was human just like everyone else. I also had a mom and a dad just like everyone else. Right up until I didn't have a dad anymore.

I was standing up in the backseat of my mom's old brown station wagon looking in the rearview mirror at her blue eyes with red swollen eyelids smudged with black mascara that was also streaking down her cheeks when she said,

"I've got something I need to tell you."

The last time I had spoken to my dad I knew he didn't sound right. Whenever he would call, my mom would always complain about it being long distance and it cost money so we never could talk long. I don't remember much about the conversation we had.

The only thing I really remember is that he sounded like my dad, but not the strong booming voice my dad had. It sounded weak and shaky. I kept asking what was wrong. After my mom hung up the phone, all she would tell me was that he was sick.

In the days following that phone call I heard my mom talking to people on the phone about cancer and chemo treatments. I heard her say that my grandmother traveled from England, Arkansas to Arlington, Texas to be with my dad. My little brain couldn't comprehend how my grandmother got there because she didn't drive and she had no car. I determined that *she took a train. Or it could have been one of those big buses like my other grandma rode on.*

Then, standing there in that backseat of the station wagon, I looked into the mirror and saw the tears about to spill out of her eyes when she just said it so matter of fact,

"God is your father now."

I still remember the confusion going through my mind and I can almost hear myself struggle to say the only word I could get to come out, "*Why?*"

I knew what she was going to say, but I didn't want her to and then she said it anyway,

"Your dad is dead."

The words hit like a ton of bricks and I couldn't catch my breath. I can still feel how hot my face got and once the tears started, my mom started begging me to stop crying saying,

"It's okay though. God is your father now."

I don't remember saying anything other than "what's going to happen now?" and back then it was hard to get me to say anything, so I doubt I said much of anything else besides that since that was already a mouthful and I already had the hiccupy crying going on. I was terrified to be in the world alone without a daddy anymore. In a futile attempt to calm me down, she said,

"You've got the best father in the world now."

I didn't want God to be my father. I wanted my daddy back. She pleaded with me to accept this life changing event as being a good thing and said,

"You shouldn't be crying. You should be happy that God is your father now."

I definitely was not happy. What I wanted to know was why God would take my dad away so that He could be my father. I was so mad at God and I definitely wasn't about to ask my mom about it. I was angry with her too. She didn't even try to console us. She didn't even look back at us. She just kept driving.

It's probably not how I would have told my three children that their father and the man I thought was my true love is dead, but it's really hard to say what I would have done. I've been in some situations where ahead of time I said I would never do the thing I did so I'm sure she was just doing the best she could with what she had. Pretty much all she had at that moment was God and us.

As a mom, thankfully I've never had to be in that situation. Little did I know then that I would have my own share of hard issues to try to navigate with my own children in tow. My little mind definitely had no comprehension of that then.

All I wanted to do at that moment was to get away from her.

We got home and as soon as I knew nobody would miss me, I ran to my hiding place. The box end of an old refrigerator truck which sat in the middle of our pig pen. The back end was sealed shut, but there was a ladder attached to the back of it so I could climb up and crawl up on the top. No one ever looked for me there. That day I don't think anyone even cared where I was except for God.

I laid on top of the end of that truck what seemed like all night wondering what my life was going to be like now that my real father was dead.

I stared up at the stars and said, "*Okay. You're my Father now.*"

God must have met me there because when I crawled back down off the top of that truck, I walked toward the old run down mobile home thinking that there was no other kid I knew that had God for their dad.

And then the big momma pig spotted me and chased me. I fell on a rock that gouged my knee open pretty good. That scar on my knee looks much smaller than it was that day. I ran to my mom crying.

She kept saying, "*I can't fix it if you don't let me see it.*"

Finally, I removed my hand. She dug out the rock, cleaned it and doused it in iodine before covering it with a band aid.

"Good as new. It'll hurt for a little while, but that's how you know you're getting better. It hurts."

I didn't like sitting with the hurt. I preferred distraction. Distraction meant that I could leave the hurt and come back and deal with the hurt once it had scabbed over. Of course, by the time I came back to deal with the hurt, a scar had formed. Don't fix what's not broken is what I did.

It never occurred to me that she might have had a dream of becoming something more than the mother of three kids living in a run down shack with a husband that ran the roads. I think when she met my dad, she started dreaming that her life would be like Johnny Cash and June Carter. She did live that life for a while, except for the happily ever after part.

That last conversation I had with my dad, my mom took the phone away from me. I thought it was because I wouldn't quit asking, *"what's wrong with my daddy?"*

I vividly remember feeling like it was my own fault I didn't get to say goodbye because I wouldn't quit being so worried about how strange his voice sounded. Her journal entry went on to say:

> **Forgive yourself for hanging up the phone when they were talking to their Dad for the last time.**
>
> **I thought they'd talked long enough. No amount of talking was going to make it better for anyone and it was just going to make my phone bill higher.**

The day of the funeral someone asked if we were going to ride in the family car to the funeral home and my mom told them no. I sat out on the porch on the swing at my grandmother's house and watched everyone leave. After what seemed like a few hours later, they took us to the cemetery and I watched while they lowered the casket into the ground. My aunt pulled some flowers off one of the arrangements and later helped me press them in a book.

My brother had gotten to go on a trip to Rhode Island in the eighteen wheeler my dad drove. He said I would get to go with him next, but he died before I got the chance to go. He was the first close person in my life to die. He was the only person then that I thought loved me the most and all the sudden he was gone. *Forever. I didn't even get to tell him goodbye. He's gone and now I'll always be stuck with her.*

One of my dad's cousins came to the funeral wearing a tie pin that looked like a pair of handcuffs. He told me he was a sheriff. My brother told me that he remembered a car full of women that were my dad's girlfriends. I don't remember that at all. I guess it's funny the little things you remember as a kid.

After reading her journal entry, I was hurt and I didn't understand why she couldn't just tell me what she did. Instead, she made me wait until after she was gone to know. In spite of the hurt feelings, I kept reading:

Dear Lord, I'm sorry.

I confess bitterness because I too was not allowed to say goodbye to my Dad. Hurt and angry and

bitter. I resented that and in my fear "never will I do that to my children" in a blindness that only You Lord can understand I inflicted this curse on them.

Can I forgive myself?

While I was letting myself travel down memory lane, I realized there are things I can't remember. My life from 9 to 12 years old is more of a blur than anything.

Some people get all upset when they think people have blocked stuff out of their minds and can't recall events that happened. Like it's some big mystery and they have to figure out the answer.

I was without a father. My mom wanted God to be my father. It seems like my memories pick back up when she married my step-dad. At least there's only 3 years I lost. My mom spent the majority of her adult life trying to recall more than bits and pieces of her childhood.

Where do I start? Do I forgive my Mom or forgive me? Do I acknowledge how angry am I or how hurt? I think so.

I felt like I wanted to ask my Dad to forgive me for letting my Mom make me lie, make me think she was good and he was bad, make me dishonor him by not giving him an opportunity to show mercy or forgiveness or whatever.

Anyway - read and write later.

Diane Beadle 9-28-1995 4:00 p.m.

Once I got to the middle of it, I didn't know any more if it was her or me writing it. Then, I wished I'd never read it, but then I realized it really serves no purpose to be angry with someone who doesn't know you're angry with them unless you just feed on being emotionally tormented. Before, I thought it was my fault I didn't get to say goodbye to my dad. Now, it just hurts to know that she carried that guilt around with her. I just wish she would've told me. I would have forgiven her. I forgive her.

After my dad passed away, my mom was able to move us out of the single-wide trailer that was falling apart in the country, into a small white house in a modest neighborhood. To her, one of the biggest selling points of the house was that it had a den with a whole wall of built-in bookshelves. At that time, it was nicer than most any house I had ever been invited in to visit, much less live.

My mom had hundreds of books. I picked out a book off the bookshelf and she took it out of my hand and handed me a different book called *The Lion, The Witch and The Wardrobe*. From that moment on I was hooked on everything C.S. Lewis. The Chronicles of Narnia became one of my life long favorites, so much so that I've probably read each book at least ten times. I've also seen all of the movies too, but I still think that the books are so much better.

If you've never read the books or seen the movies, you won't understand some of this, but sometimes I would wish so hard that there was a secret wall in my closet that would let me escape into a different world like Narnia. It's funny how even as an adult, every time I see a lampost, I still wish for that sometimes.

I've often thought about my mom's experience almost like stepping into Narnia, the way Lucy did. Except when my mom "came back," time had passed, things had happened, and the world wasn't the same. Or maybe I was the one in Narnia, watching her shift, disappear, reappear, trying to make sense of what was happening. She believed she would go away and another version of herself would step in to handle life. Looking back, I'm not sure she wasn't simply just trying to survive the only way she knew how, using the patterns she'd learned to cope with pain.

It's hard to put into words, but I think I understand her more now because I've done something similar myself. When life presses too hard, it's easy to slip back into a version of yourself you don't want to be, not quite as joyful, not quite as peaceful, not quite as gentle, but at least able to function. When my mom got angry, she could be complicated and unpredictable, and I've had to face the hard truth that I can be the same way.

When I get angry, there are moments I can't fully remember, not because I'm unaware, but because the emotion buries everything else. If someone walks me back through what happened after I've calmed down, the memories return. And every harsh word that comes out of me in those moments usually traces back to something buried, something I've been holding onto, something that finally erupts. And once the moment is gone and if it isn't talked about, it can fade from my mind as if it never happened.

It's strange, but I'm beginning to understand what she was wrestling with. At first it terrified me. I thought it meant I was "crazy." But my mom did things that looked chaotic, not crazy. She was a woman trying to survive more than anyone ever knew. God gave her a sound mind, even if her life didn't always look that way. And He gave me a sound mind too.

The one steady thing in her life was her faith in God. No matter what she struggled with, she never denied Him. And for all the confusion and pain and complexity, that is the gift she handed down to me, a faith that holds, even when everything else feels like it's slipping away.

CHAPTER 9

I told my mom once that I wanted to be like Amy Grant and have a singing career. She gave me the short answer of no, you'll get addicted to drugs and sex. I told her that I was a Christian and wouldn't do that. She told me that I wasn't Christian enough not to let that happen so I didn't need to pursue that dream. Well, apparently I wasn't Christian enough not to let that happen despite having zero fame and fortune.

I didn't listen to her, like with most things, and I pursued that dream regardless of her wishes. I found out Star Search was doing auditions, so I signed my thirteen year old self up and then begged my mom to take me. It never occurred to me that she might have been taking me with the idea of, if I would do this and fail, then that would be that. It also never occurred to me that she thought I was good enough to make it. Well, I didn't fail. At least I didn't think I failed. As a matter of fact, I got to go back for a second audition and then I got to wait anxiously, for what seemed like eternity to a thirteen year old, for the mail to come with news if I'd made it on to the third round or not.

I spent hours in my room practicing. I wasn't the kind of girl who sang into a hairbrush in the mirror. I was the kind who imagined the full stage setup—the heavy mic stand that I would lean into, grabbing the microphone only for the dramatic effect when the bridge hit.

I had the song picked out perfectly: *You Better Wise Up.*

When the envelope arrived, my whole body was literally shaking as I slid my finger under the sealed flap. I pulled out the letter. I had made it to the next round. The finals.

All I needed was the $249 entry fee.

It could have said I was one of 200 out of 2,000, but my memory feels more like it was 20 out of 200. There were a select few that had been selected to come and have their audition videoed and submitted for the final round of auditions. The catch was it was going to cost $249.00. Well, it may not have been exactly that, but it was two hundred and something that my mom said we didn't have.

I called her on the phone. My hands were shaking trying to dial the number. I don't remember whose house she was cleaning that day, but she was cleaning somebody's house. There was always a list next to the phone of the days of the week and the names and numbers of the people whose houses she cleaned underneath the day she cleaned them. She answered the phone and I told her what the letter said. "I can't afford it. End of story."

I couldn't say anything back. If I did it meant I was getting three swats with the paddle when she got home. That was if she remembered. It was one of the good things about her that I counted on sometimes. Of course, trying to get all my chores done and done right may have helped some I'm sure.

This is one of the few memories I actually let myself recall so many times that I thought I had finally convinced myself that it was all a scam and my mom was right. I would have ended up a homeless prostitute somewhere in the dark scummy places of Nashville. The truth is that I went from believing I was good enough to, actually trying to get on Star Search to meet Ed McMann to, it was a stupid idea anyway to, my mom is probably the only one that thinks I sing good, to how could I have really believed I could sing. So, I switched my thirteen year old dream to designing album covers for people who could sing, namely my best friend at the time who, shocker, isn't a famous singer now either.

My thirteen year old self did lay in bed and contemplate whether or not it would be worth it to sell your soul to the devil like I was told rock and roll singers did, but in the end I decided that even if I could, I wouldn't have. I think at that age I had a pretty solid relationship with God. Then along with another birthday came rebellion. That is when "the talks" began.

Over the years my mom's diagnosis would change from multiple personality disorder to dissociative identity disorder. Her personalities would be called inner children, inner parents, altars and eventually have their own names. People have asked me what my mom was like when I knew she was my mom and not some alternate person. Truth be told, it's hard to know for sure, but I think the one thing that I knew was my mom was in constant communication with God.

It's hard to remember a time when I lived at home that my mom was just sitting down relaxing, watching TV or reading a book. Even though she had a long list of chores for us kids to do every day, which included the laundry and starting dinner, she was always busy doing something. It never seemed like we did the chores the way she wanted them done so she would have to go behind us and fix what we didn't do right while she yelled at what all we had missed or done wrong.

My brothers and I would start doing things like throwing the silverware in the trash. Our reasoning was if the silverware wasn't going to be clean enough for her, then why bother trying to wash them. It was easier to just throw them away and deny any involvement when she figured out it was missing. It wasn't long before we only had about 4 forks, 2 spoons and 36 butter knives left in the drawer.

When we started doing this our silverware drawer was overflowing. One day she opened the drawer and then started digging through the sink of dirty dishes looking for silverware. It was hard to deny what had happened at this point so I told her we did it because she could never find just one thing that we had done right. That did not end well for me. I felt like she did try to make an extra effort to point out a thing or two I did right over the next few days, but I finally figured out waiting for her to pat me on the back was just not going to happen and there wasn't anything I could do about it. If I complained, I got in trouble. The best thing to do was to accept it and find someone else who thought I did a good job.

My mom told me once to be careful not to break someone's spirit. She said you can get to the point where you're so mad at someone that you can beat them down so bad that you'll change them and you'll never get their love back. She told me this during a conversation we were having around the time when I was a pre-teen or a teenager.

TCBY (This Can't Be Yogurt) had just opened and she and I would have what she called "Mommy Daughter Dates" and what I called "torture therapy". We would go in and get our yogurt and then go sit in the parking lot in the car and she would talk while I tried to eat in spite of her ruining my appetite and my treat by making me so miserable listening to her.

During one of these talks I thought, *does she even know me?* The talks were usually about things I hadn't even thought about doing yet, like smoking cigarettes and doing drugs, and hanging out with friends that were described as horrible people. I didn't even know they existed because I didn't have friends. She would talk about how I was going to get myself involved in situations where I would prostitute myself out and on and on about the other horrible things I would do and I could just sit there and wonder *why the hell is she telling me this?*

Once I cried so much that she told me she was sorry she had to tell me things, but she did it so I would be stronger. It reminds me of the time when she told me that every time she hurt me it helped me because the next time it wouldn't hurt so bad.

I was the best example of a good church girl or a goody two shoes within a 100 mile radius. My whole reason for living was to not be a disappointment to my mom. After that first trip to TCBY and experiencing the first of what would be many "*talks*", I would absolutely dread hearing her say, "*Do you want to go to TCBY?*" How could I tell her no? She would say it like it was going to be such a fun thing for us to do and she had saved extra money just for me.

We would get home and sometimes my step-dad would ask if I was all right. The person I had been stuck in the car with acted like nothing had happened. Thinking about it now, I do remember that sometimes she acted confused about why something would be wrong. Sometimes she would even ask me what was wrong, but all I could do was look at the floor and say, "*nothing*" and then go in my room and shut the door. Fortunately for me, I could take a short walk from the front door and two rights and be in my room.

I guess she thought the frozen yogurt was supposed to make the talks we had better, but it didn't. My appetite was ruined every single time and every single time I had hoped that maybe it wouldn't happen this time. Because we were so poor, restaurants, much less fast food places, were a luxury we didn't get to indulge in very often so when I got to have something like that, it was special. Until I learned the price I had to pay for it and it had nothing to do with money.

Unfortunately, I dreaded these dates so much that all I could do was buckle up and ride it out, so I mostly only remember the dread. I cried. Alot. I feel like the Beetle in this journal entry was probably my step-dad, but it feels a little like me she's talking about.

Dear Diane, Telling you how I feel is hard for me. People crumble and cry when I feel. They can't bear my hurt. They can't feel secure when I feel. Here is a story for you.

Once upon a time there lived a little bitty ant.

This ant was always very busy and trying her best to keep everyone happy.

One day a big beetle came into her world from a place called fall apart easy.

Even though he was big, he could fall apart easy, so ant had to be very careful not to bump into him when she was working.

He came and told her he wanted her to be happy
but when she'd try, he'd fall apart.

So finally, she just gave up.

So that is all of the story.

What could we do to help the little ant?

Put the beetle outside.

How can we do that? He lives here.

I've read this story over and over trying to figure out who or what she was talking about. When I read it as if I was the one who wrote it, I think I understand a little what she was trying to say. The best I've come up with so far is that the beetle came along and wanted to live with the ant because he saw how happy she was.

However, when the beetle found out the ant relied on Jesus and that's why she was happy, and that in order for him to be happy he needed to rely on Jesus too and not on her, every time he tried, he would fall apart.

I understand how difficult it can be to live with someone that doesn't understand how you can trust God. I've trusted God that when enough felt like more than enough, that was enough for me.

She used to tell me *if you know you have a bear, then why on earth would you want to poke it?* I wonder if her beetle in the story grew into a bear.

CHAPTER 10

My life from 9 years old to around 12 years old is kind of fuzzy, just like my mom said hers was, but what happened one day at the Pentecostal school I began attending the fall after my dad died, is still vivid to this day.

I was sitting in chapel and the pastor, who was also the principal of the school, was talking about water baptism. By this time, Shiloh Tabernacle, the church we had been attending, had split up and we were part of the congregation that started going to a different church, which I'm sure is part of the reason I ended up in a different school.

But, before that happened, I had been water baptized at Shiloh and according to the pastor at the Pentecostal school, I had nothing to worry about and was on a clear path to heaven. Later on in my life I'd run into a Baptist preacher that told me since it was performed by a reformed Catholic that it probably didn't count, but just so everyone's minds are at ease, don't worry I got baptized again not too long ago just to make sure the world knew I wasn't going back!

My mom's personality for the most part, if you left her alone and didn't say anything to her or get in her way, would be pretty calm and she would either be singing or carrying on a one-sided conversation with God. However, if you wanted to talk about something that made her uncomfortable, which talking about my dad or her mother always made her uncomfortable, she would become anxious and the more anxious she became, the more animated her facial expressions would be and her voice would change and the conversation would pretty much become one-sided because you couldn't get in a word.

My dad had only been dead a little over a year and I knew that people went to either heaven or hell when they died. I thought they told you whether the person that died went to heaven or hell at the funeral and as hard as I tried to remember, I couldn't recall if the preacher said one way or another about my dad as they lowered him in the grave.

When I asked my mom about it, it was during one of those times she was singing and praying. She glared at me for a second and then softened her eyes. She said that my grandmother had told her that my dad accepted Christ as his savior just minutes before he died so he went to heaven.

The next time I saw my grandmother, I asked her about it, but she just looked at me confused and told me she had prayed with him before he passed. I wasn't much of a talker when I was young and I'm sure this was one of those times they regretted ever begging me to talk.

So, back to the chapel at the Pentecostal school. I was pretty sure my dad wasn't water baptized and I shared this fact with the pastor. The pastor told me that since my father wasn't water baptized, he went to hell, just matter of fact like that.

Well, after having a meltdown and the staff at the school not being able to console me, they finally gave in and called my mom. She came to the school and picked me up from the office. Once she got me home and calmed down, I told her what happened in between bites of a scrambled egg sandwich.

Scrambled egg sandwiches were on the short list of things my mom actually cooked well. I'm still not sure how she managed to mess up so many other meals, but somehow she did. Anyway, one time when the church decided we were all going to "fast and pray." I was seven or eight, trying my best to be a good little church girl and, as usual, trying to win my mom's approval. So I announced that I would fast and pray with her.

I don't remember how long I lasted, but I know it wasn't more than a few hours. What I *do* remember is that my fast ended with her making me a scrambled egg sandwich. To this day, whenever I need comfort food, that's still what I want.

When she fasted and prayed, she sometimes did it for a solid week or more. It always amazed me how devoted she was when it came to anything like that. But looking back at pictures of her during the years she was anorexic, I can't help but wonder why no one stepped in and said something. Maybe they did. Maybe she just didn't listen. Or maybe, like a lot of things in our family, everyone thought it was "between her and the Lord."

It was okay that they told me we were sinners because we wore makeup, cut our hair and wore pants, but apparently, telling me my father went to hell was where they crossed the line. There have only been a handful of times I've ever heard my mom so mad that she would cuss, and this was one of those times.

She told me we were going to march into that school, I was going to get my things and I would never go back there. Her rebel personality took over that day because when I asked if it would be okay for me to take off my dress uniform and wear my pants inside the school, I saw fire in her eyes when she said, "Absolutely!" Any other time she would've said that wasn't a good thought for me to have.

It couldn't have been long after that when she enrolled me in Cloverdale Christian Academy. I was the new kid transferring in mid-year, but some of the kids I went to church with also went there, so for me it was a better experience all around. It always amazes me how people can remember what teacher they had in what grade, but for me the only teacher I can recall is the one I had at that school, Ms. Atchley.

The next year I skipped 7th and went straight into 8th grade. Ms. Atchley was my teacher again. I was thrilled. The school only went through 8th grade and at the end of the school year, my traditional school life would be over. I was not thrilled about that.

Truth be told, I was devastated. I was finally able to escape a few hours a day from the craziness at home and feel like a somewhat normal kid. Now, everything that was normal was being taken away. My brothers were allowed to attend public school, but my mom was adamant that I would either go to a private school or be homeschooled. Even though she said I would not attend a public school, she did have some pity on me because someone told her about a magnet school that I might be able to attend, and she took me there to try to get me enrolled. In the end, she said there were issues that kept me from being able to go and ultimately, she made the decision that I would be homeschooled.

She gave me a big thick workbook that said GED on it. Apparently, she didn't look at it close enough because all the answers were in the back of the book. I did complete what I could on my own, but if I got stuck, I had the answers right there. I don't know if she thought I was really smart or if she was relieved that she didn't have to try to teach me. She had only finished 8th grade herself and she never was much help when it came to helping me with my homework. Anyway, she gave me the workbook and said when I finished it, I was done with school. Fortunately, I took it upon myself to learn things myself and I actually studied different things on my own outside of that workbook.

I spent all day by myself. She and my stepdad worked. My brothers went to school and I stayed home alone homeschooling myself. You wonder why teenagers think that they know more than their parents. Well, at 13 years old I came by it honestly, I think.

The rules for dating were only group dates at 14 which meant it had to be at least 5 people. Double dates were allowed at 15 and no single dating until I was 16. Needless to say, I followed the rules long enough that it appeared to her that I was following the rules. That usually only took about 30 minutes after leaving my house. Of course, those weren't the only rules. The other rules were no hand holding because hand holding led to kissing and absolutely no kissing because kissing led to sex, and you were not allowed to have sex before you were married. If you got married, that would be the person you would be with until one of you died, no matter what.

I didn't know then that she had divorced my father. What I did know was that I didn't trust her to tell me the truth. I had already caught her lying about when she married my dad, and I had walked in on her and my stepdad having sex before *they* were married. Then one Sunday I heard a sermon on hypocrites, and in all my youthful boldness, I told my mom that's exactly what she was. I knew it hurt her feelings, but she was always so matter-of-fact about everything, and I was just telling her the truth in the only version of love I understood at the time.

It was frustrating to be constantly preached at about doing good and staying on the straight and narrow, only to watch her swing wide and act like it was no big deal. To my young mind, it felt like she was holding me to a standard she wasn't even trying to keep herself. I didn't have the maturity then to see the fear and shame underneath her choices. All I saw was the contradiction, and it made it hard for me to believe anything she said.

I found a journal entry that gave me a little insight into the years she spent growing up.

5-20-95 On our way to Gilbert Park

11:00 a.m. Writing about my feelings. The music is kind of a distraction and Robert is asking did I remember this or that, but hopefully it'll drift off and I'll be able to start really expressing how I feel.

I know that I had some really feeling feelings this morning as I was waiting on the Lord. I know a few days ago that this trip would be like going to church again for the first time after a move as my scenario has been faithfully unfolding itself as I've been feeling through each day. Feeling the feelings the best I could ahead of time was nothing like knowing this morning where we

were going to go. I thought I remembered some of the shame and disgrace and cried some, but not oh, not near enough.

My family was so dysfunctional. My embarrassment of them haunts me now. Rather than coming in feeling whole and well, glad to be back with friends that we had told we were leaving, I felt disgraced. Maybe because we'd lied to them again. Said we'd never see them again. We were moving to Iowa.

This seems like a re-entry into the California church. Although, I'm sure now it was the other way around and probably was just as traumatic. But Southgate held stability whereas Iowa didn't I don't think.

My Uncle John was part of the problem with California I think. We were accepted graciously on his behalf I think. They held him in high regard. He was special even before he became a millionaire. He must've been well to do even before that.

My first remembrance of Uncle John in California was when I was in second grade I think. I remember kindergarten, all three schools. First grade and second grade become more blurred. Third grade was Southgate I know at least once. Second or first Atlantic, Iowa school where I got in trouble for saying I'd come from California.

I think the time we waited in his driveway for them to wake up before we woke them was the time before that. Then it's possible the time for me to witness was during this time and then we moved to Iowa again. It was during that time I realized Uncle John was esteemed highly and we, Mom and I, were esteemed highly because of him.

Yuck, so lets say go to Iowa, do the 1st or 2nd grade in Iowa. Winter – Uncle Milton dies – Atlantic, Iowa – church Dad pastors – different houses – school there I go back to and not accepted by my very good friend. Really got bad reception all through that. I was new to the town, to the state. Was made fun of by kids and so on. Glad to change schools.

11:30 Talked to Robert about my feelings. Love Robert so much. Thank God for Robert. Somebody loves me enough to listen to talk and share my feelings.

1:00 Feelings – I hope that the knowledge that I am not a misfit, that I am a citizen of Christ's saints will help me feel like being myself and fit in. Well, fit in as being able to feel real and myself and not have to worry about what people think about me or my family.

They may not like me. What God has said about me is what counts. My feelings about my family go tight, then release. Somehow I guess I could freeze it all and make us all disappear.

When we would go to church I would feel so uncomfortable knowing everyone must know how odd my parents were. But we were not odd. We are not any odder than most folks. Brothers and friends and alot of them have moved all our lives. He always transplants with "care" and only when necessary and vital to the work of His Kingdom.

Hope, peace, faith in seeing with my well heart, not my sick heart. I believe.

5-21-95 Going Back

2:00 p.m. Well, alot of enlightenment came I

think about my illness. There seems to be just an ever strong desire in my sick heart to feel shame and guilt.

As a figment of my imagination "I'm sure" Amy was jealous and protective of Ray.

I've talked to Ray a few times when I've called to talk to Amy and he has given me "scripture" and I mean scripture to meditate on that would have to do with my problem as he saw it.

Everytime afterward I've checked. Anything I said wrong? Anything he said wrong? No. Maybe it was because I hadn't gotten a chance to talk to Amy right before we came but I had talked to Ray about how I felt like I had leprosy and ought to be an outcast of the camp.

He said he didn't know any of us that weren't a broken mess and that if we were going to wait until...

Stopped and talked to Robert about my feelings now start back.

2:21 p.m. But he's turned the music on. Oh well –

It's harder for me to write how I feel when music is playing but I can write about experiences of past feelings and so on.

I remember going to a water spicket and getting water and remembering the Tennessee experience. Also trying to wash dishes in wash basins instead of a sink. I felt the usefulness of a mission and the liking to do a little more difficult task that could otherwise be done be indoor plumbing.

Kind of like I feel when I get down on my hands and knees and scrub a floor with a brush instead of using a machine. I work so slow when I clean anymore. I wonder if the medicine that would help me stay focused would help with my work. The medicine might cause the clearness I need in my mind to receive the enlightenment and help from the Holy Spirit to cease. I really would want the Holy Spirit to give me an answer about that.

Anyway back to feelings at church.

If I knew my Mom was cheating on my Dad, if I knew it or even just sensed it, wouldn't I feel ashamed and uncomfortable when going to church?

Especially if I was in the Helen's daughter mode – taking on the feelings of uncomfort for Helen, thinking I guess that it helped her. I don't know. Maybe thinking that if I could stay in tune to what she was feeling I could stay ahead of not doing something that would embarrass her. Cause she would say "I wish I could die" if I embarrassed her.

During the night I laid awake wanting to sleep. I grabbed my head. I grabbed my hair. It was like a baby in despair who couldn't speak what it felt. Just wanted to not be there. Felt unable to really feel the feelings cause they were to unspeakable or expressible. Didn't want to be held or loved. Just wanted to be gone.

It was like my reflexes or understanding of what I wanted or needed were backward. You know as a little baby left unattended did surely it would want to be held.

But I didn't even though I knew that was what I should've wanted or needed. I wonder if a chemical imbalance could cause this in me even as a baby. My knowing of absent love was there. I was unable to accept that anyone would love me. And that I was capable of loving. Did not feel I could love or could be loved. I'd say during the night I was Baby One mode. When I woke it was hard to say who I was. I tried hard to feel the feelings. And think what is expected of me. What do I want to do? Went to take a shower while someone in our group watched Brittany for me while I did.

It felt good to be clean.

4:22 We stopped and looked at Wooly Hollow State Park. Now on the freeway going towards Little Rock.

I wonder if the time that Al's wife came and yelled at my Mom had anything to do with anything. When he had a car wreck, Mom went to Riverside to see him in the hospital. She took me and Donna too. Think she got caught because of someone seeing us. Can't figure out why she wanted us to go and see him.

Life for me at age 12 became a blur. My mom who pretty much ran my life was running away from me. While the freedom from control was something that I wanted, I couldn't visualize myself able to function at all without her help. She told me when I made social errs. She told me when I needed more smarts when it came to choosing friends.

So when one girl had decided to choose me for a friend I didn't know how to deal with any way except to say what my Mom had said about her and that she wouldn't make a good friend for me. I was totally shocked to realize this hurt this girl's feelings. And when my Mom (when I told of course) found out she said,

"You would be stupid enough to tell her that."

My Mom's cross out standard's for blessing was never something I could catch on to as being something wrong with her. It was always me. And when it became damned if I do and damned if I don't. I just chose non-existence. No friends. No life. No hope. No joy. Till I'd get a clue that there was something else I could try that might work. Cause no friends wasn't what she wanted for me.

So, I'd try. But what kind of friend did she want me to get. I never got friends like she had told me. She said I should choose friends and not let friends choose me. Maybe that meant all those people who wouldn't look at me or say hi to me were the ones she thought I should have for friends.

That was a scary thought. How do you get to be friends with those people? That must not be it. I tried making a friend with someone who went to church.

Isn't Neomi a strange girl? And her and sister said Tom and Joe would come and spend the night at their house sometimes.

I couldn't quite figure that out, but she went to church. Surely. No. Really Strange.

Diane, can't you find some more friends?

Shirley went to church.

But she's Mexican Diane.

That did it! I thought you said Jesus loved all the people no matter what color?

This time I knew she had to be wrong if it was because she was a Mexican. Besides Shirley had picked me.

Other people I had to confront and break the relationship I'd just used what my Mom said. But that didn't work too well. People got really hurt and angry so this time I knew she was wrong.

So I just thought I'd be her friend in secret. Well, she had six Mexican brothers who of course my Mom wouldn't want me to be their friends either so I just wouldn't tell her and we would be friends in secret. Not all six. Two. One at a time.

Oh well, I was getting all the coaching from a mother whose husband had divorced her for adultery. But do you ever think that occurred to me? No. Divorced for what? Cause my Dad and her couldn't have sex and she couldn't stand it anymore.

Not good enough to take care of us though. My Dad had us. All 4 of us. But she was around all the time. To tell me what to do. Course she was busier now. Didn't have as much time to know what I was doing.

Life was life and I wished it would go away. How

could I have any fun. And to make matters worse they'd stopped moving from town to town. Oh they moved from house to house to house to house. But there was just one Jr. High for the whole town so friends and teachers didn't change.

My life was miserable. Both parents controlling. I'd have to sneak out to have fun. Life was awful. And when my Dad married Bertie life was absolutely awful.

And then Christmas was coming and my Mom wanted to take us to California. Don't tell Dad you are not coming back. It was either betray her or betray him. And we all hated Bertie. But I don't know if she told Donna or the boys. They loved their Daddy you know. I bet they wouldn't have gone.

I remember the total gratitude I had for someone finally doing something on my behalf. It was like wow you mean you really give a flip about me? And I was so glad.

But in California things didn't quite go right. And before I knew it how dare I betray her? Betray her? What did I do that made

her think I'd betray her? She seemed really under condemnation in California. Whereas in Colorado she'd been okay.

Now it seemed she couldn't have a good day. And it was my fault. Little betrayer. And we couldn't get along. She just kept doing weird stuff. Going to church and dating married guys.

Diane Beadle (undated)

I really loved my grandmother. Whenever she would come to visit, at the slightest mention that we were hungry, she would make us something to eat even if it was past our bedtime, telling my mom we shouldn't go to bed hungry. I can really only remember a handful of times that she came and visited. It was the same way with my mom's father and her siblings. We didn't see them often, but when we did I was always excited to see them.

Up until the family breakup, that's what I call it anyway, my grandmother always sent me a card and money for my birthday with a letter to my mom telling her to let me pick out something nice for myself. I always mailed her a letter back letting her know what I bought with my birthday money. Even after I was out of the house she continued to send me letters and cards for my birthday.

When I had my first daughter, she mailed her a dress. Three months later she asked my mom why she hadn't heard from me thanking her for the dress. I didn't realize that the key I found in my mailbox was to a group of lockers that held packages that wouldn't fit in the mailbox.

Once I figured that out, I found the dress. Fortunately, she had bought it too big and by the time I got it, it fit her perfect.

My mom and my grandmother would write letters and send tape recordings of themselves back and forth to each other all the time. About once or twice a month, they would talk by phone on Saturdays when the rates were down. If money was tight, they would resort to more letter writing or more taping. When I cleaned out my mom's house, I boxed everything up and put it in storage with the old yellow suitcase. Years later, I started going through all of those things and came across many of the letters my mom had saved that my grandmother had written her.

I thought my mom was so mad at my grandmother and that she was convinced it was my grandmother's fault that she had multiple personality disorder. The last 25 years or so of my mom's life she had no communication with her at all. Whenever I tried to talk to her about it, I never really got a straight answer why. Sometimes she would say it was because my grandmother thought my mom was being brainwashed by her therapist and other times, she would say it was because my grandmother refused to speak to her because my mom left the church. Sometimes she would say that she wanted to see her, but my grandmother refused to talk to her. I believe it was all of the above.

I can vividly remember the last phone call I had with my grandmother. At the time, I was living in Benton, Arkansas, with my girls who were three and five years old. The telephone hung on the wall in between the kitchen and the living room. It was white with a long cord that would nearly reach all the way to the front door in the living room. The girls and I had just recently taken a trip to Iowa to visit her. She called to see how we were doing and told me that she had just gotten off the phone with my mom. My mom had told her no more phone calls. She could write her letters, but there was no guarantee that my mom would read them.

My mom would eventually put even stricter boundaries in place for my grandmother. Those boundaries were evident in the letters that my grandmother wrote my mom. It was also evident that my grandmother didn't understand why my mom had to go digging in her past and couldn't just let it go.

I did try to keep my relationship with my grandmother a secret from my mom, but my aunt let it slip to my mom that my grandmother and I had continued talking. So, grandma and I got a phone call from my mom and then I got a phone call from grandma, and then that was that.

That last conversation with my grandmother ended with her explaining to me that she couldn't have a relationship with me because my mom didn't want to have a relationship with her. For many years, I thought it was because my grandmother was mad at my mom, which meant she was also mad at me. I also thought it was probably her way of controlling my mom by trying to use me to try to change my mom's mind about talking to her. In the end I decided that she just didn't want to do anymore damage to my mom than she felt she already had.

That conversation, combined with the knowledge of the letters she wrote my mom during that time, it is evident that it wasn't me or my mom my grandmother was mad at. She really was just trying to do everything she could for my mom to get better. If that meant giving up having a relationship with me, she was willing to do that, but I don't think it was as easy of a choice for her to make as I once thought.

Near the end, my mom decided that she wanted to go see my grandmother. There was some disagreement with others in the family over my mom's intentions, but I believe she just really wanted to see her mother one last time. My mom bought an airline ticket, but before she was supposed to fly out, her pain from the cancer went out of control and she was put on hospice care. There was no way she could physically go.

Time had run out and she would not be able to make that trip. From what I've been told, my grandmother had dementia for several of the last years of her life and didn't recognize any of her family, but I really think she was waiting on my mom to come see her. She died two weeks to the day after my mom died.

I found a letter my grandmother wrote my mom. I was going to just pull out some pieces of the letter, but after sleeping on it and praying about it, I decided for a slew of reasons to let you read the whole thing.

April 17th (1995) - Monday evening 7 p.m.

Dear Diane, I received your long letter today (this evening) when I came home from work. I worked a extra hour at restaurant today, was supposed to get off at 3 and today was tax day, so the owners went to finish their taxes and didn't get back until 4. I had planned to be in Shiloh by 5. I sent you a letter Saturday telling you of my plans to be in Shiloh this week. Well, I hurried home from work and changed clothes and as I was hurrying to the car the mailman came. I sat in my car and read your letter. I read page 1 and debated about praying on the way to Shiloh before reading the rest -

but no, my trust is in the Lord that no matter what your problem was or is, it was okay for me to go ahead and read. When I finished I thought, isn't it wonderful that I didn't get this letter til today. The letter I wrote you Saturday telling you how the Lord told me He loves you more even than I do and reminded me how special you are. I think that that letter should mean more to you by mailing it before I received your letter. Because at the end of your letter you tell me, quote, I fear, I fear to love. I fear to be loved. And how you let "fear" know it can't have dominion over you, etc.

To me just knowing the Lord loves me, cancels out any fear of loving or not loving. As long as I have his love, then I'm free to love with His love flowing thru me. Example. This elderly lady (85 years) that I care for, was very nasty to me the 1st day I worked for her. I went home and I prayed. In my prayer I asked the Lord to fill me with love for her. He (the Lord) helped me see that her stroke has affected her mind and he just flooded me with love for her. I didn't have to tell her I loved her, it comes thru in the Spirit. When I left that day, she took my hand and said, "I love you."

I don't know if this means anything to you or not. I'm probably missing the point of what you're trying to tell me. All I know is, when I sat down to write you that letter, I had no intension at all in writing you what I did. I was just going to write a short 1 page letter and tell you I'm okay and what my plans were for the week (this week). To me, knowing the Lord loves me, well, that's all that matters. In the past 6 months I'm being lead into a relationship with Him, one step at a time. It's a growing experience and hard to explain, but the foundation of it is, there is a trust established between us. When I now say, I know He does all thing well, I know I really mean that. Every prayer is answered. Maybe not the way I wanted it answered, but knowing its the way He wanted to answer it. I bet none of the Apostles ever expected to end up in jail when they went out and ministered the good news that we can have salvation by believing in Jesus and his blood being shed for us. But they not only ended up in jail at times, but they sang songs and praised the Lord while they were there. They must of had a trusting relationship too, huh?

I know the Lord is going to, not only going to, but is taking care of you. I know He loves you because He told me so. I trust Him completely. I trust Him with you and all yours. I trust Him with Donna, Bob, James and his family. If I looked at it from the natural, I'd say, God what is going on. But I'm not saying that. Each of you are going thru things.

As for moving every 3 months - It wasn't always your Dad. It was me too. Your Dad had to be busy. He moved and painted and papered and fixed a place all up and the he moved again. He couldn't sit down at night and watch TV. He or myself never ever thought about the fact that our kids had friends in school or maybe lied the house or place we were at. We never every thought about you. I know I loved you. When we were still married (except the last 2 years) I thought I was a good mom. Our folks never discussed with us moves or anything that affected us as a family. I guess they were the Dad and Mom and we were their property. That's the way things were in the old days. No one ever questioned it or even thought about it. Now, we find out we were all dysfunctional families. Now I'm 66 years old. All my children are grown. All of you have problems. All of it goes back to your childhood. You, Donna and Bob anyway. James don't seem to have problems like that. He's pretty happy with the way he grew up. He told me when he was 19 years old and it was a Father's Day and we were having coffee, and he said "Mom, you always felt you never gave me a Dad. Well, I grew up knowing God was my Father and when I had a problem, I went and asked Him what to do and He told me, so I wish you wouldn't feel bad anymore.

"But the thing is, I can't do anything about you being raised in a dysfunctional family now. I was raised in one too, but the only way that affected me I guess, is I'm different than all my brother and sisters and I don't fit

anywhere. But I don't have time to spend on it. I'm not gonna get down and dig out all the roots of it all. At least I'm not until the Holy Spirit tells me to. I know He must have told you too, or you wouldn't be doing it. I don't suppose I'll ever have a friend type relationship with anyone or that kind of thing - but it's okay for me - because I'm different from everyone else. Time I work 2 jobs and wait on the Lord - there's no time left in a day to give a human type of relationships.

Well, I guess I'd better close. I'm at Shiloh and it's 8:19 p.m. Service starts at 9 p.m. cause it's a phone patch from Sepulveda and it's only 7 p.m. out there. I got to go shower. I'll reread this in the morning. If I mail it, it will be because Holy Spirit said its okay. Probably not help you, but it has helped me. I love you and I bless you with His blessing. Mom

P.S. Next day. I prayed. As far as I can tell it's okay to mail. If not - tear it up and forget I wrote it. Then tell me it upset you - so I can be sure next time.

I thought this letter was probably one of the last letters my grandmother wrote my mom that she actually read. After their relationship became estranged, I saw my mom tear the letters up that she got without even opening them.

When I was really little, all the way up until I was an adult, they exchanged letters. It wasn't the typical way you would think people exchanged letters. You know, you write a letter and send it to someone. They get your letter and write you one back. You get their letter and you write them back and so on. No, my mom and my grandmother wrote to each other several times a week as they felt like it. And those were just the letters that actually got sent. I came across a couple of them in the suitcase that my mom wrote my grandmother and didn't send. At the end of the letters it said, "If you're getting this letter it's because the Holy Spirit said I could send it." I guess the Holy Spirit must not have said she could. After I read them, if I was the Holy Spirit, I would have said, "Nope!" They were rough.

After I read the letter from my grandmother, the more I understood where my mom thought the personality of Helen's Daughter came from. My heart ached for both of them. I know my mom said some pretty mean things to my grandmother. There's no telling what else my mom said to her and my grandmother said to my mom that I don't know about. I sure hope they're both up there in heaven and have gotten it all sorted out.

Understanding that letter opened a window into my mom's inner world. I finally saw why she clung so tightly to the personality she called Helen's Daughter. It wasn't just a name she made up; it was the only version of herself that felt safe. For the first time, I could see the little girl inside her, the one who had been wounded long before she ever became my mother. And that letter made it painfully clear who my grandmother had been in my mom's story, both her source of strength and her deepest wound, a woman carrying her own brokenness long before it ever spilled onto my mom.

By the end of her life, she wasn't a maze of personalities anymore. She was mostly herself, still imperfect, still complicated, but softer and steadier than she had ever been. But in 1989, neither of us was anywhere close to healed. We were both still a mess in our own ways, stumbling through confusion, fear, and a whole lot of unspoken pain. And my life was about to take a turn that no workbook, no personality, and definitely no Holy Spirit–approved letter could have prepared either of us for.

CHAPTER 11

My mom really never had much to say about her life from the time she was five until she turned about seventeen. Mostly what she told me was that they moved around quite a bit. She would get settled into a new house and a new school, but before she could really make any new friends, they were moving again to a new town.

When I was a younger mom, it seemed like I had started down that same path of moving from here to there, but once my kids started school, her talking about how hard it was on her to change schools came back to my mind. I didn't want that for my girls and I probably made some decisions that wouldn't be considered in the best interests of anyone, for the sake of keeping my girls from having to move around. Of course, my mom was not shy in telling me what her opinion was about the decisions I was making, but the problem was she never had any good solutions to my problems, but I digress. This story isn't completely about me. It's mostly about her.

So as I was saying, I didn't know much about her life from five to seventeen. I've been told how my grandparents owned cafes and my mom would mingle with the customers when she was little. I know very little about her teenage years except that her parents were divorced, remarried and living in different states. From what I can gather from different sources in the family, our family wasn't so different than all the other dysfunctional families that I've seen over the years. What's heartbreaking is that there are some that, even fifty years later, still feel like they need therapy to get over it.

Which led me to my next realization that it doesn't matter if you are or aren't so different from everyone else, it still hurts when relationships fall apart no matter who you are or what age you are. Ask me how I know and I'll tell you that God created me with a natural desire for relationships and I can't imagine that particular trait could only be unique to a few.

After she passed away, I came across several pictures that I had never seen of her ranging from when she was a small child to a teenager. It's a little eerie looking at the photographs because the hairstyles she was wearing in those pictures seem very similar to the different hairstyles she would try to see if they would suit her personality. I also wondered why she never shared her pictures with us.

After I became a teenager, my mom was adamant that I could go on group dates, but not real dates until I was sixteen. I could have a boyfriend, but I could not hold hands. Holding hands led to kissing, kissing led to sex and sex was something reserved for marriage. She swore to me that she didn't have sex until after she was married. Then, I walked in on her and my step-dad before they were married so I knew she was not telling me the truth.

That began my new hobby of snooping. I learned that papers weren't just labeled important papers for no reason. They were things like marriage licenses from previous marriages. Namely, the marriage license for when she married my dad in 1975. My brother was born in 1971 and I was born in 1972. This whole pre-marital sex talk she gave me was even more suspicious on top of seeing her actions. I knew it had to be the whole do what I say and not what I do, but after a few weeks I had convinced myself that my mom wouldn't lie to me about having sex before she was married, so the only logical conclusion was that I was adopted.

Finally, I got brave enough to tell her that I knew her secret and wanted to know who my real mom was. She admitted that she had hidden the truth because she didn't want me to do the same things she did and think my life would turn out okay because her life turned out okay. I was devastated partly because she really did lie to me and partly because there was no birth mother to go find and move in with. It was the only time I could ever remember telling my mom that I hated her and the only time she ever slapped me across the face.

It would take me forty years to realize that at that moment in our life, she really did think her life had turned out better than she could have ever dreamed it would. I'm not sure when she finally let go of her dream so God could give her a better one, but it had to be years before I was standing there with a red cheek, because the one thing I was sure of was that she thought her life was pretty good and up until then, she had me convinced that it was too.

The questions I was asking about my life back then were the same ones my mom once carried in her own heart, even though I only knew her as a grown woman still holding pieces of that younger version of herself. It wasn't until much later that I realized we both started down the road toward total independence at the very same stage of life, almost like we were unknowingly living some kind of a weird parallel existence.

As an adult, I can look back and see that this fierce independence was something I picked up from her. It wasn't a flaw. It was simply a part of the uniqueness God gave us both. But when we pushed away from God, that same independence opened the door for chaos, because what we were really craving wasn't independence at all. It was the freedom to live the way we were created to live, with God as the One we lived for and our families as the ones we cared for, because He cared for us. Somewhere in the midst of the chaos it got all jumbled up. She was pushing away from the chaos towards God. I was pushing away from God and towards the chaos.

One of the few things she did tell me about my dad that bordered on being bad, was that she always thought that he was seeing another woman at the same time she was pregnant with my brother. She wanted me to know that because she thought the woman had a baby and that I could possibly have a half-brother out there somewhere. I'm guessing with the age of computers and my snooping abilities, she didn't want it to be another shocking experience for me if I did happen to come across him.

Another thing she didn't tell me was that on March 10, 1967, at barely seventeen years old, she married Earl J. Schleper in San Bernadino, California. I had no idea she had been married prior to being married to my dad until after she had died. Apparently, not even successfully hiding parts of her life she didn't want me to repeat, stopped me. I also got married at barely sixteen. I used to call it fate, but now I'm convinced it was a family sin or generational curse that just needed to be broken. Fortunately, God heard my prayer and that pattern was broken in my family starting with my girls.

The day after she died, I decided it was time to close the chapter on her life and make it Ancestry-official. I typed in her date of death, and immediately a little green leaf popped up. *Would you like to see a new hint about your mother's past?* Why yes, yes I would. In hindsight, they really should give you an *Are you sure?* button. Maybe even a *Why don't you think about this before you click okay?* button. But they didn't, so here we are.

That hint led me straight to a name I had never seen before. Earl J. Schleper. Because I'm me and because once I have a question I want the answer immediately and I know how to do that really well, I found a phone number for an Earl Schleper and called it right then. His new wife answered and then handed the phone to him.

That was when I learned that my mom had broken Earl's heart. He was nineteen and she was seventeen when they married. He told me he came home one day to find that she had loaded the car and the boat with all her things, and all he could do was stand there against a tree while she drove away. When he said he never really knew what he had done that was so terrible, he sounded sincere.

That was the last time he ever saw her, and he hadn't heard a word about her life since. He finally divorced her in June of 1969. When I told him she had died, he cried. It was hard to imagine that someone out there had carried such a deep love for her that it moved him to tears, especially when I hadn't even grieved for her myself at that point.

Once I convinced him I wasn't his long-lost child, I told him he had actually gotten lucky. She ended up being crazy, and I didn't know why. That was the whole reason I had called him in the first place. I promised her I would write a book about her life and I was trying to find answers about what "they" had done to her and I didn't blame him. He was just someone who happened to be standing in the path of her destruction at the wrong time. Eventually, though, that path of destruction shifted into a path of life, because somewhere along the way I came along, and she stopped blowing up relationships and swung to the opposite extreme, trying too hard to hold on to every single one.

Come to find out my dad was not a saint either. He was married to Betty Taylor until 1973. Unfortunately, Betty passed away before I found out about her. I did get into contact with Betty's sister who assured me that Betty and my dad did not have any children. I like to be thorough with my investigations and she gracefully redirected me. She told me that my dad was a really good man. I think she might have just been trying to be nice because I wasn't naive. I was a year old when he divorced Betty. He would not have been my definition of a good man.

Before it was stolen, the only thing I had left to remember my dad by was a gold lighter engraved with "Love, Linn." At the time, I didn't even know who Linn was. I only learned her name later when I saw it listed as his spouse on his death certificate, thanks again to that little green leaf. That's when I knew my dad had remarried before he died. I think I might have met her once, but I never knew she was my step-mother.

This is probably as good a time as any to tell you about my mom's house cleaning business. When we first moved to Little Rock from England, Arkansas, she got a job working at the Vagabond Inn as a waitress. This would have been around the time I was seven years old or so. One of the regular customers that came in started getting to know my mom. I'm not sure what all she told him, but I'm sure it involved her having three kids at home and being a single mom. She probably left out the part that they were home fending for themselves while she was there working.

It really doesn't matter how it happened. The good thing is that it happened because that meant my mom became an entrepreneur. Mr. Beavers was one of her last customers to wait on at the Vagabond Inn and her very first house cleaning customer. He asked her to come and clean once a week for him and his wife because they had gotten older and he didn't want his wife to have to work so hard. I wondered if *my* dad wanted *my* mom to work so hard. He probably didn't, but he had other things that had his attention and that didn't leave her much of a choice.

I don't remember the circumstances that made way for me to meet Mr. and Mrs. Beavers, but I'm guessing they figured out we were home fending for ourselves and instead of calling DHS, they helped in ways they could and because of that, I will probably never forget them for as long as I live. Not just because of what they did for me, but because of what they did for her. Life finally started looking up for my mom and because of that, it started looking up for me too.

She started cleaning their house weekly and I visited with them weekly. It wasn't long before I started getting their granddaughter's hand me downs. At eight years old, I don't remember owning any dresses before the ones I got from her. If I did, they certainly weren't near as nice. They started referring my mom to their friends and their friends referred her to their friends. Word must not have traveled fast enough because before I had turned ten years old, she had my brother and I sitting at the table, going through the phone book, highlighting phone numbers that had the prefixes that belonged to "the rich people".

At first she was only brave enough to call the "455" numbers, but later she got brave enough to call the ones that started with "224". As we found the numbers, she would call them and introduce herself and ask if she could come give them a quote for cleaning their house. She paid us a nickel for every phone number we found that she called and the people answered. We would ride with her and wait in the car while she went in and looked at their house and gave them a quote. She was always happy when she left their house because they simply gave her hope of cleaning their house. She was even happier when she left knowing she had a new customer and we got 50 cents.

It was also around that time that I realized my mom was trying to come to terms with her own childhood, her trauma, and everything therapy was stirring up. And because of that, she started bringing up memories from my life too. These were memories I hadn't felt any need to revisit. The past was the past. I had survived it, buried it, and moved on. My Grandma Burkett once warned me that people do not like the skeletons in their closets disturbed. I understand that firsthand now. When someone starts dealing with their own buried memories, they start wanting you to dig up yours too.

My mom was a single mother until I was twelve, and we really did live in a rundown trailer with holes in the floor big enough to fall through. But despite what she later claimed, she did not stay moral or "not date" for two years. She may not remember it, but I do. There were nights I crawled out of bed and walked down that dark hallway, stepping over the dining room table leaf she used to cover the holes, only to find her entertaining a man. Once I was spotted, I would get the usual, "Go back to bed, I will be there in a minute." I must have always fallen asleep before that minute ever came.

There was one night I got up to use the bathroom, flipped on the light, and found a man sitting on the toilet. I screamed at the top of my lungs, thankfully not one of those dream screams where nothing comes out.

My mom came running, scooped me up, and started yelling, "*Get out. Get out of my house!*"

She told me later someone had broken in, but I never knew if that was true. All I knew was that from then on, I associated a man I sometimes saw at the grocery store, an old man with a pointy hat, long white beard, and walking stick, with the man on the toilet in our house.

After she had been in business a few years and after we had moved from the run down trailer off the side of the Interstate into a modest home in a subdivision, the newspaper came and did a huge article on her and her business. She was so nervous, but she did what she taught me so well to do. She put on a smile and winged it, acting like it was no big deal and that being a maid was certainly not something to be ashamed of like my peers tried to convince me it was. The article came out on the front page of the Society section and right next to the article was a big picture of her dressed up in her uniform.

It was a one-piece beige jumpsuit. Not at all like the black dress with a white apron the other kids insisted she probably wore. No one knew that starting out she could only afford just one. At the end of every workday, she washed it, ironed it and got it ready for the next day. She didn't want people to think being a maid was a demeaning job for poor people and even though she was poor, she was not going to look like it.

She was one of the first people in Arkansas to start a house cleaning business and it wasn't too long before she was hiring other women to work for her. This was before Merry Maids and other maid services were a thing. I like to think that Merry Maids actually got their idea from her. I mean it is plausible, right? She got so upset because a few of the ladies that worked for her actually went out and started their own house cleaning businesses taking with them the houses that she had assigned them to clean. She upped her game and made anyone that came to work for her sign contracts that they wouldn't compete against her and take the houses she had worked so hard to get. Some of them still did it anyway.

It was one of the few times she seemed so genuinely confident and humble and sincerely shocked that she was a person of interest to the news, much less society. I can't recall her ever trying to draw attention to herself. More than anything she strived to slip in and slip out of the public unnoticed. It's another trait I learned from her that comes in handy sometimes.

I, on the other hand, was upset that she had actually become famous while I was still embarrassed of her. The kids I went to church and school with would laugh and say her dream job was to be a maid in a fancy French maid outfit, flirting with her customers. I told them she wasn't "just a maid." She told me she professionally cleaned houses, and I repeated it like it was a badge of honor. Then I added that they were just jealous their parents couldn't afford her to come clean their house. The truth was, she felt like a big smudge on the picture of my life. I wasn't upset that they were making fun of *her*. I was upset that they were making fun of the fact that my mother was a maid, like I had any control over the career she picked. If it had been up to me, she would've been an Italian supermodel or Mrs. Beaver. I just didn't want her to be my mom.

As with everything He does, God used her cleaning houses to give her a best friend. One of the women whose house she cleaned for years ended up becoming one of her closest friends. I don't think either of them would have picked the other on their own, but I'm convinced God picked them for each other. My mom always told me that God would give you the desires of your heart, and what she wanted more than anything was a true friend. He gave her one.

From what she told me, and from what I saw, my mom felt like she brought something more to that woman's life than just cleaning her house. She helped her organize and helped her tackle the little tasks that felt overwhelming because of the emotional storms her friend was walking through. And my mom needed something too. She needed someone she could share her faith with, someone who made her feel, if only for a few hours each week, like she was normal. Their friendship mattered deeply to both of them, and in time it grew to include another woman who became part of their small circle. They poured so much of themselves into those relationships. They knew God had placed them in each other's lives because they truly needed one another.

There were plenty of people at church and from her past who considered her a friend, but she struggled to believe they really were. Part of it, I think, was that she believed people were friends with one of her personalities, and she wasn't always sure which one. She didn't know what she might have said that she couldn't remember later. Somewhere along the way she'd been convinced that forgetting something you said wasn't normal. I sure hope it is, because I do it all the time.

I always thought that if she had told people about her multiple personality disorder, the people she could have been friends with would have understood her situation and become good friends with her. Instead, she ended friendships because she was scared people would figure it out. Many of those people were left thinking they had done something wrong, when all the while it was nothing at all that they had done.

Her multiple personality disorder was something I believe the enemy tried to use to convince her it was a death sentence, something that would destroy the relationships that had finally become valuable to her. In the end, she may not have had many relationships, but the ones she did have were deep, steady, and real. They were the kind of relationships I can only hope mine resemble, something more than surface-level, something more than just people passing through each other's lives.

She really was an amazing person. I think her soul was just shattered into a million pieces. She would start with a flash of a memory, and once her mind started going down that rabbit hole, the emotion would build until it was too much. It was just all too much. Ask me how I know.

CHAPTER 12

Every morning for as long as I can remember, my mom would be up at 5:30 a.m. to "wait on the Lord." I always assumed she got up that early so she wouldn't have to worry about being bothered by us. Being a single mother of three and later four kids, one of us always needed her for something.

I say she did it for as long as I can remember, but honestly, I don't remember her doing it until after we moved into our new house and life started looking a little more normal—less like we were straight out of the Ozarks or "the hills," like my mom's family called my dad's family. But once we settled into that house, she never missed a morning that I can remember.

Knowing what I know now about her past, I think she may have been trained to "wait on the Lord" from a very young age. I've read stories from others who were involved in The Walk or The Living Word Church, and it seems that was a common thread. The children in that church were woken up before dawn to wait on the Lord, and as an adult, she reawoke the practice—assuming she had ever stopped in the first place. Her first waking moments, her first thoughts, her first words of the day, she reserved all of it for Him.

I tried giving God the first fifteen minutes of my day, but it just felt like I was checking Him off my to-do list. But if I had never felt that way, I don't think I would have understood why she did what she did. Now I'm starting to understand. It wasn't an obligation for her. She did it because she needed God's guidance and wisdom. She didn't want her prayers to be in jeopardy of falling on deaf ears, so she must have wanted to stay close enough to God that she knew He would hear her.

In addition to waiting on the Lord, she would go into her room at any point during the day to "intercede in prayer" for people. When this happened, we were given strict instructions not to interrupt. It only took one time for us to realize she wasn't kidding.

I don't remember which one of us was brave enough to knock on her door, but I do remember the door flying open and her looking like she had just breathed fire. We stood there smoldering and slightly singed, grateful to have only been yelled at and spared from the paddle.

She did have a paddle. It was one solid piece of wood about an inch thick, six inches wide, and eighteen inches long with a handle. My brother will swear it isn't true, but he discovered power tools and got the bright idea to drill holes in it.

Anyway, back to my mom and her praying. She was serious about it. If she prayed for you in Arkansas and you were in Alaska, you knew it without even asking. In fact, if she knew you, you didn't even have to ask to be prayed for. She prayed for you whether you wanted her to or not. If anyone on this earth had a direct connection to God Himself, it was my mom, and you'd be hard pressed to find someone who would disagree with me.

She kept getting up early and praying until she physically couldn't anymore, not long before she passed away. I asked my sister if I was remembering that right, and the way she cut her eyes at me and raised an eyebrow told me nothing had changed even after I moved out.

My sister is my sister, but if we're being petty, she's technically my half-sister. My mom married my stepdad when I was twelve, and they had my sister when I was seventeen years, three months, and eighteen days old. I couldn't believe how careless they had been, so I added it up. It was before we had computers, so that's probably why it so clearly stuck in my head. Of course, I eventually let it go and had to recalculate/google the exact number for the book.

My mom stayed married to her dad until he died, but they did separate when, as he put it, living with her was too much for him to endure while trying to hold on to his own sanity. Of course, he wasn't without fault. Years after they separated, she told me she had caught him cheating on her. This was right at the beginning of cell phones, and we were not the kind of people that could afford cell phones, so when she said she caught him, I'm pretty sure she didn't mean she caught him talking to someone. She really caught him.

Long before that happened and before dinner one night, I had taken a shower and wrapped myself in a towel and wrapped my hair in a towel. I was a teenager, but it was common for me to take a shower, wrap myself in a towel and walk across the hallway to my bedroom.

When I came out of the bathroom that particular time, my stepdad was standing there. He asked me if I knew where a board game was. He followed me to the back bedroom, and I pointed up to the shelf in the closet, showing him where the game was that he was looking for.

Before he reached up to get the game down, he kissed me on the forehead.

He had never been affectionate towards me before except for maybe the occasional sideways hug, and I don't really even remember hugging him then. My own mom rarely hugged me and she sure didn't ever kiss me.

My whole being cringed. A new worry that I never had to worry about before came to live with me. I wasn't sure what would happen if I told my mom, so I just didn't say anything.

We sat down at the table to eat dinner, and I asked my mom if she could take me to the mall so I could hang out with my friend.

Before she could answer, my stepdad cut in. He told me that from that point on, I needed to okay going anywhere with *him* first.

I looked at my mom and said, "*He's not my dad. You are my mother. You tell me what I can and can't do.*"

Apparently, what little leverage I thought I had over my stepdad, I didn't. There was no doubt it was the wrong thing to say because my stepdad picked up his plate of spaghetti and threw it against the wall.

The plate hit the wall and fell to the floor. The spaghetti made a big red splat, and the noodles slid down the wall.

I looked at my mom's face. It was just a total blank, and then she started to cry. She really never cried unless she was praying, and that was okay. However, if you saw her reaction to a situation was to cry, you knew it was time to go to your room and just stay there until the storm blew over. It wasn't often, but you always knew she felt different about you afterwards, and that wasn't always a good thing.

I had moved to my own side and asked her to leave my stepdad's side and come over to mine. It was a terrible place for me to put her. A place

I wouldn't understand until years later when my own kids would put me in the same place. But that day, I knew that he wasn't my friend or my parent, and my mom, she couldn't be anything more to me right then than a name bearer. Mom.

We got to have the nice house, the nice car, and all the food in the fridge because my dad died. She didn't consider the price she would make us pay so that she could have a companion, just like I didn't consider the price I would make my own girls pay so that I could have a companion. We all got broken and hurt in the process.

That day, I think in order to try to keep damage control to a minimum and keep major changes from happening, we all just tried to forget it happened and let things go back to what was a normal existence.

Unlike with *my dad*, there was no packing of suitcases this time. There was no running away in the middle of the night. We just cleaned up the sauce and went back to pretending we were normal.

Normal existence for me had been going to school and going to church and hanging out with friends on Friday and Saturday night. But since finding out that the parent-child relationship I thought I had with them had just been shattered completely, I stopped believing in the illusion of my normal existence and started scheming ways to make my life better than what it was by getting away from them.

He never touched me again, and neither of us would mention it again until several years later.

Still, I knew something just wasn't right. I wasn't one to talk too much because the less I said, the less I was noticed, but my mom's behavior had finally bothered me so much that I couldn't hold it in anymore. I finally asked her why sometimes she was so different when we were at church, and then when we came home it was like she was somebody else.

My stepdad and my brothers stopped what they were doing and turned their heads to stare at her, waiting for her answer. They had to see what I saw. Surely I wasn't the first one to just say it that straightforward to her. I was just a child, but it was obvious that I was the bravest one of the bunch.

She laughed and said, "You just watch, I'll be me all day today."

It wasn't that she was nice at church and mean at home—which she was, but not unlike everyone else's mom. It was just that she was undeniably, distinctly different towards different people. At church she would be a version of the mom on *Leave It To Beaver* and just overly nice to people I wasn't sure she even really liked. At home I can't even begin to think of who to compare her to because it just depended on the day and her mood.

It was weird, but she did manage to pull it off that day. It was the only time she really did seem normal. She wasn't too uptight. She wasn't too laid back. She wasn't too nice and wasn't too mean. She was just... normal.

We didn't have church that night. I'm not certain if they were having what they called "home group" and it was her night to host it or if she was entertaining friends, but what I do know is that we went to church and then came home and had lunch before we started cleaning up the house. Normally she would be shouting orders and telling us we missed a spot or didn't do something the way she would have done it, but she didn't. Instead, we got complimented on how good of a job we did and that never happened.

I told her a few days before that all she did was point out everything that we did wrong and never told us we did anything right. The first gasp she let out should have been all that I needed to stop, but I kept going. I told her that all she could ever see was everything bad I did and complained about it.

Then, right before her face got too red, I told her that I was going to go pray that Jesus would tell me what to do to make her happy because she wasn't doing a good job of explaining it. I wasn't sure what her face looked like after that because I was retreating into my bedroom to "*pray*" for her as I was saying it.

I'm sure a grounding followed, but when you don't have much, you don't have much to get grounded from. It was usually having to go straight to my room anytime I was home, except for dinner and the bathroom, for a week or two. It was where I was more than happy to be because if I wasn't grounded, that's where I was anyway.

That day I was grounded, but allowed to be in the room with the company we had at the house. I kept waiting for it to happen. She told me that she could do it and if I was going to prove her wrong, I had to pay close attention. I kept waiting for her to fly off the handle and lose her Jesus over the smallest thing not going exactly as it should, or suddenly flipping a switch and being the perfect hostess who was just a little too nice and smiling just a little too much.

But this time she didn't. She just maintained.

I wasn't paying that close of attention because I didn't notice my mom had left the room until I saw her walking back in the room carrying a white laundry basket that I kept stuffed animals and other things I wasn't supposed to in. It didn't surprise me that she went to get it, I just wished she would have asked *me* to go get it!

There was a small child that had come to our house and she brought it in there to give him something to play with. Of course, instead of taking the animals out one by one and giving me time to get over there to fake being nice and playing with him, he dumped it out. In front of everyone.

All I could do was cower and just stand there waiting to see what my mom's reaction was going to be.

Out with the stuffed animals fell my pack of cigarettes.

She literally just laughed and said, "Oh, she's probably just hiding those for her brother who is going to get it when he gets home!"

Who was I to argue with that kind of logic? Even after everyone left, she never blew up. She never stormed in my room and demanded to know the truth. She just took my cigarettes and probably smoked them even though she was a former smoker, but she never spoke of it again.

At that time the song *Father's Eyes* was very popular. I had sung it a couple of times at church as a "special" and I had just begun this eye-opening walk with Jesus. It seemed like up until then my relationship with Jesus had been more of a father-daughter relationship, but now He had become this friend that understood everything about me.

I told God that I didn't understand why she didn't get mad, but I figured He had something to do with it.

There were other nights I can remember lying in bed crying, just pouring my heart out to Him. Even though there were some rough things happening in my life, I believed every word of what I sang to Him. You couldn't have convinced me that anything would ever creep in and make me doubt those words. But eventually I would doubt again and trust again, like a pattern I kept repeating for the next forty years.

CHAPTER 13

When my mom first told me about her multiple personality disorder, I was an angry twenty something year old who had finally been vindicated by receiving confirmation that she indeed was right, her mother was crazy, but even long before that I didn't understand why out of all the people in the world I had to be the one to end up being born to her. I was probably still a little upset over the whole not being adopted thing. It's okay to laugh. Sometimes that's the only way to keep your heart from breaking into a million pieces, but at some point I think you need to cry. Eventually, I run out of tears and weirdly feel a little better. I realize now how blessed I was to have her as my mom because she taught me everything she knew about grace and overcoming. It also put me on a journey to process some of the things that no child should ever have to deal with.

We had traveled up there to visit my grandmother, who lived in Kalona. Both she and my mom were still deeply involved in the Living Word ministry, and my grandmother attended services at Shiloh religiously until she physically couldn't anymore. To them, it was just a normal family visit, so naturally, she took us to tour the complex.

That is when the threat became real.

Walking those grounds, I thought it was rather odd that everyone else saw this place as normal. I saw children out in the fields working in the massive gardens, shoveling manure where they kept the livestock. They looked like little adults, stripped of their childhood.

What stands out in my mind more than anything was the basement. Down there, rooms were filled with bunk beds for lots and lots of children, ranging from twelve to eighteen years old. There were massive storage rooms filled with food that had been canned from the garden those same children worked. The whole place pretty much ran itself, well, with the help of those kids who were my age and older. It had its own water tower, huge gardens, livestock, and a massive auditorium for church meetings that was packed full when we visited.

So later, back in our kitchen in Arkansas, when my mom looked at me and threatened to send me to Shiloh, my blood ran cold.

It wasn't just a vague threat or a name on a map. I knew exactly what it was. She wasn't threatening to send me to boarding school; she was threatening to send me to a prison where my own grandmother would watch me scrub floors and shovel poop. I stood there thinking about that farm in Iowa, knowing I didn't know a soul there. If she sent me away, I would be working for strangers hundreds of miles from anyone who knew my name.

Fortunately, and most likely by divine intervention, she changed her mind and did not send me. Even though she may have thought she did not know how to love me, I have no doubt that somewhere in her heart she did. Also, that divine intervention could have something to do with the time I was kidnapped or the time I ran away. It was the same incident. You would just have to see it from a few different perspectives and decide for yourself what you want to call it.

As an adult, I think I could be justified in not admitting any wrongdoing in a situation like that where people that are older and should have known better could be blamed. However, I cannot deny that I did have a part to play in it and I will tell you what part that was.

We were living in Little Rock, Arkansas, and attending church in Benton. At around nine years old, I began to blossom early and by the time I was twelve years old, I truly thought I was grown. There were just a handful of things I needed to figure out and then, I was pretty sure I could live on my own, without my mom. When the incident happened, I was working on figuring out all of those things, but I was not quite ready.

The church we were going to had a big youth group and I participated in just about everything they did. I became friends with a girl there that was several years older than me and I did what most girls my age did and told my new best friend everything about my life.

This was long before my mom was diagnosed with multiple personality disorder so that secret couldn't be told.

Instead of complaining, I was constantly trying to come up with a solution. At that time, my solution to making everything right in my life, was to get away from everything that was wrong.

It wasn't long after the "spaghetti incident" and the trip to Iowa that I had decided I just couldn't be in that house anymore and I started thinking about running away. It could have been months in the development stage, but I feel like it was probably only a few weeks. All I know is I had pretty much chickened out and had decided to put it out of my mind when my friend called on a Tuesday and said, "tell your mom you're going with me to the church to help babysit."

She had decided this was the perfect opportunity for me to run away. She didn't tell me where I was going or what I was going to do. I didn't have anything packed. While I was waiting for my friend to come pick me up, I wrote a note explaining to my mom that I couldn't live there anymore.

By the time I had finished the note, I decided not to leave it for her. I folded it up and slipped it in my back pocket as I was walking out the door to get in the car with my friend. All the sudden running away didn't seem like the right solution, but all I can really remember for certain is that I felt like the bars were about to be opened and I was going to escape.

As we were driving, I asked what plan she had devised for me to run away. I don't remember much about what she said because I was starting to panic as she pulled up next to two men in a truck. She told me to get out of her car and into their truck and said she would see me later. My next thought was *how am I going to get out of this?* I had been on trips out of town before with other people, but they were always people that I knew. These grown men I had never met and did not know and I was terrified. This was before cell phones and tracking devices and GPS so there was no way for anyone to know where I was. For all my mom knew, I had simply vanished.

The two men drove me to Jacksonville, Arkansas. I don't remember much about being there, but I do recall getting there. There was construction being done on the interstate and there were cones set up to keep people from driving in one of the lanes. The man that was driving decided it would be fun to weave in and out of the cones going down the interstate. At that point I thought, *this is it. They are going to get pulled over and I can go back home.*

The truck smelled like stale cigarettes and old grease. I sat sandwiched between them, praying my prayer of invisibility, trying to make myself as small as possible. The radio was blasting something loud, heavy metal or rock, and every time the driver jerked the wheel to swerve around a cone, he laughed. It wasn't a funny laugh. It was an evil laugh that made my stomach drop.

Well, they didn't get pulled over even after running down several of the cones. That evening, they drove me to Southwest Little Rock and pulled in the parking lot of an apartment building about 3 miles from my house. We got out of the truck and walked up stairs and into an apartment. It was neat and clean.

There was a girl there, probably in her twenties, that was visibly upset that they brought me, a child, to her apartment. One of the men told me to sit on the couch and watch TV. I sat down, but I couldn't concentrate on TV at all.

All I could think about was what was going to happen when it was time to go to sleep. I made up my mind that I was not going to fall asleep. Once everybody else was asleep, I would sneak out and walk home. When I was six years old, my brother and I used to walk a mile down the side of a busy road with no sidewalks to the grocery store to buy candy. It wasn't unusual to find us playing outside until way after dark. I figured if I could survive that, I knew how to get home from where I was. I could survive a few mile walk in the middle of the night. I could go back home.

The only problem was I didn't factor in what their plan was for me. The other man and the girl that were there went into the bedroom. I was sitting on the couch and the other man walked over to where the light switch was on the wall. He told me to take off all my clothes.

The air left my lungs and it felt like I couldn't suck any air back in.

As I started pulling down my jeans, tears started rolling down my cheeks and he turned the light off. In the darkness, he told me to lay on the floor.

As I started to crouch down to lay on the floor. There was a loud knock on the door and I heard the words.

"POLICE. OPEN UP."

The man flipped on the light and threw my clothes at me. He told me to get dressed and tell them I was eighteen. I got dressed as quickly as I could. Barefooted, I walked into the kitchen on the other side of the door and stood next to the counter. He opened the door and two men in police uniforms pushed their way into the apartment.

I looked down at my toes.

One of the policemen walked up to me and in a kind voice asked how old I was. I told him I was eighteen, just like the man told me to do.

Then, he said, "what year were you born?"

No one had told me how to answer that question. While I was trying to decide what year I had to be born to equal me being eighteen years old, the other men were being put up against the wall and patted down. It was then that I reached around and felt the note in my back pocket.

If they patted me down and found the note, then they would just think I was a stupid runaway that deserved to be in trouble, but I didn't run away and I didn't want the girl at the apartment to be in trouble because of what I had done.

I decided the best thing I could do for her and myself was to slide my note under the dish towel that was holding a draining rack on the counter. I figured that she would find it when she was cleaning and be able to show that it wasn't her fault.

After the policemen patted down the other men and put them in handcuffs, their attention turned back on me.

One of them asked, "*Did you ever figure out what year you were born? Someone called about a noise complaint and we found you.*"

All I could do was look at him with tears rolling down my face. He said, "*Let's get you home.*"

They took me to the police car and put me in the backseat and drove me home. As we pulled up to my house and I got out of the car, I could see my mom on her knees through the big picture window of our living room. When I walked through the door, she let out a huge sigh of what I can only imagine would have been relief. She told me that when she came home and found me gone, she got on her knees and told God she wasn't getting back up until He brought me home.

My mom was clearly happy for me to be back home, but there were no big hugs and no questions right then about why I would do something like that. That would come later. She asked how I got home and I motioned to the policemen outside who were pulling out of the driveway.

Once I was in my room, I laid down in my bed. It would be years before I would sleep in anything other than my clothes. While I was laying there, I thought about everything that had happened that day and knew that from the time I walked in that apartment, it had been totally quiet. The girl had insisted that I stay quiet. The policemen never asked me my name, my address, my phone number, or who my parents were. They simply drove me home, opened the car door for me to get out and left.

The next day I told her some of the reasons I wasn't happy being there. She told me not to worry and that she would pray about a solution. It wouldn't be until I was an adult that I would tell her the whole story about what happened.

That's when she told me I shouldn't have been carrying around the guilt from running away, that grown people should have known better and that it wasn't my fault. Most people that have heard my story about running away agreed with her, but condemned her for allowing what happened next.

It wasn't her fault that I didn't want my friend to get in trouble.

My step dad decided it would be best if I went and stayed with my friend for a few weeks. Yes, that same friend. I wasn't stupid. I knew you weren't supposed to tattle on your friends, but I did think that the adults should have been smart enough to put together that she had been the one that picked me up that morning. During my stay with her, she would have the same men come to her house. I would sit in the truck, parked down the street from her house and smoke cigarettes while my friend and the man walked down the street. It wasn't long before I decided I didn't want to live like a rebel anymore. I just wanted to go back home. Although the situation was not ideal, it was much better than where I was. I got so homesick that I honestly thought if I didn't go back home, I wasn't going to make it.

I finally tattled on her. If her parents couldn't see what was going on, then I had to open their eyes so I could at least get back home. I'm not positive that incident caused some sort of division in our family and the church, but I'm sure it didn't help. All I know is, that phone call from her parents to my mom ended our friendship, but it got me back home. Not too long after that we started going to a different church.

I read that the Shiloh complex was burned to the ground in a controlled fire in 2019. The official story was that they were annexing the building, but reading about the smoke rising over those 200 acres felt like watching a wound finally being cauterized.

It didn't surprise me when the stories came out of abuse, control, and files kept on members. It turns out that the terror I felt as a kid wasn't just my imagination running wild. My twelve-year-old gut had picked up on a darkness that the adults were trying to call "holiness." When I saw that they had to burn it down to move on, I realized I had done the same thing by running away. I had to burn that bridge to save myself.

There is one theme through just about all of my mom's journals, she believed that she was unloveable. She thought she did not know how to love and it even applied to knowing how to love her children. I found a journal entry my mom made called "The Road Back to Honor". Honestly, I wasn't sure what she was talking about so I thought I should look up the definition of honor to help me better understand what it was she was trying to say.

Honor - high respect; great esteem; adherence to what is right or to a conventional standard of conduct; something regarded as a rare opportunity and bringing pride and pleasure; a privilege.

I didn't realize until much later that the shame she carried had quietly shaped the way I carried my own. I didn't have the same exact story she had, but I learned the same instinct to hide the parts of myself I thought would make people look at me differently. For years

I believed that if anyone knew the whole truth about me, they would only see the worst parts and miss everything God had changed.

But shame has a way of convincing you that your past is still happening, still defining you, still hanging over your head like a verdict. It took me a long time to understand that my past is just that, my past. It happened. I can't rewrite it or undo it, but I also don't have to drag it around like a punishment. God never asked me to.

Somewhere along the way, He started showing me that the very things I wanted to hide were the things He wanted to heal. And once He healed them, they weren't sources of shame anymore. They became evidence. Proof that He can take what was broken and make something whole out of it. Proof that Romans wasn't just a verse on a page but a promise lived out in my own life.

I don't tell my story because I want anyone to feel sorry for me. I'm not a victim of anything that happened in my past. I'm an overcomer. God has blessed me, strengthened me, and steadied me in ways I never could have imagined. I'm okay. I'm more than okay. I'm free. I'm not ashamed anymore, not of who I was or what I did or what I didn't know then. God has made good out of all of it, just like He said He would.

Honestly, at this point in my life, if someone wants to judge me for something I did twenty years ago, they're going to have to take a number. I've got kids, a husband, a nonprofit, and a whole community to keep up with. I barely have time to judge myself, much less keep track of who else is trying. Besides, God already settled the matter, and He didn't even ask for my opinion. He just healed me.

So I'm choosing to live like someone who's not hiding anymore. My past can stay where it belongs, and I can walk forward without flinching. If anything, I'm grateful. Those old mistakes taught me who I don't want to be, and God showed me who I actually am. If that means I get to help someone else drop their shame too, then all the better. I'll take that over pretending to be perfect any day. Perfect sounds exhausting. Free sounds much more like me.

CHAPTER 14

I didn't end up in Iowa. Instead, we left that church and found a different church. It was supposed to be a fresh start, my cousins went there, and I was ready to settle into a new routine.

I was still trying to figure out who I was. *Was I the good girl or the bad girl?*

I tried the *good girl* route first, but I went about it in the worst way possible. It was during an altar call, one of those solemn moments where everyone's heads were bowed and eyes were closed. The preacher was moving down the line, asking if there was anyone we knew who needed prayer.

When he got to me, I leaned in close. I wanted to be very *spiritual* about my concern.

I whispered in his ear, "*My cousin needs prayer. She is having premarital sex with the deacon's son.*"

I watched the preacher's face turn blood red. He didn't know what to do with that information. He just mumbled a quick prayer and hurried along to finish out the rest of the line, probably terrified of what I might say next.

I didn't get away with it, though. I got confronted immediately after church. We had a massive family meeting about it, and I had humiliated my cousins and their parents so badly that I'm pretty sure they actually quit going there.

The irony, of course, is that not long after, I did too with the exact same boy.

And unlike my cousin, I didn't just get a family meeting. I got pregnant.

That positive test was the official end of my childhood. At sixteen, I was suddenly a wife-to-be, preparing for a baby I desperately wanted, with a boy I thought I loved.

A visit to the doctor's office was so rare that I wasn't even sure what to do when I got there. When I walked in, I told the lady at the desk that I needed a pregnancy test. She took me back into a private room, had me pee in a cup, and then left with the cup. When she came back, she told me what I already knew. I was pregnant. She also proceeded to tell me I had options and tried to hand me some brochures.

I waved away the brochures and looked her in the eyes. As convincingly as I could, I told her I didn't need any options, I would be keeping the baby. As I walked out, I knew that was exactly what someone in my situation was supposed to say, but how I really felt about it was completely different.

There was no waiting to tell my mom. The baby's father was going to tell his parents, and I knew if I didn't break the news to my mom, they would. My stomach was in knots knowing the news was going to devastate her. She did not want me following in her footsteps, as she had reminded me so many times, and I had led her to believe her parenting was working. In a few short hours, I had to work up the courage to tell my mom that her "perfect child" was the one who had become the hypocrite. Her response was not what I expected.

"You know you're going to start getting sick in the mornings, right?"

She wasn't even mad. Not at that moment anyway. For once in my life, I was actually glad she was the way she was. I didn't get yelled at or preached at. She sympathized with me and even tried to be my friend. Of course, it didn't last long. The next day she told me his parents were coming over and we would be discussing getting married.

Over the next couple of weeks, she went back and forth between me getting married, sending me away, putting the baby up for adoption, or her adopting the baby herself. Eventually, it was decided that I would get married. I don't recall having much of a say in anything. The only real alternative was moving up to Amish country in Iowa with my family, and I loved them, but I knew I didn't want to live that lifestyle. I was in the worst trouble I'd ever been in, and there was no talking my way out of it. At that point, I figured I didn't know as much as I thought I did, and the adults must know what was best.

In the meantime, I just knew I didn't want to be pregnant, but choosing one of the options I'd been given would have gone over worse than getting married. If my mom had encouraged me to have an abortion, I honestly don't know that I wouldn't have taken advantage of it in that moment. There was controversy over abortions then, but nothing like there is now. My sixteen-year-old mind couldn't see the future consequences, but at the time it seemed like a solution that at least deserved consideration. I entertained the thought, even though it wasn't a decision I would ever end up having to make.

The day before the wedding, she finally presented me with a choice. She told me, *"You can leave and get married, but you can't come back home if you do. And if you don't get married, you're going to disappoint a lot of people."*

I didn't know it then, but it was the first of many dilemmas. Living with my mom had become exhausting. It always felt like damned if I do, damned if I don't. I know I didn't always make things easy, but it really seemed like living anywhere else had to be better than where I was. One thing she taught me was to let my yes be yes and my no be no.

In other words, don't threaten me to get your way, and if you're me, decide what you're going to do and do it.

She was the one who instilled that in me even to her own detriment. Surely she must have realized it as I packed the few belongings I had. The next day I stepped into day one of my adult life.

In nearly every picture of the wedding, my face is a pure blank. There was no emotion. Even now I struggle to remember the details, because it wasn't a day I wanted to remember.

I saw my Grandma Burkett, my dad's mother. I didn't even know she was coming, and when I saw her, I wanted her to tell me she had come to take me home with her, that this was all just a big misunderstanding and everything was going to be okay.

She just looked in my eyes and smiled, patted my hand, and told me how beautiful I looked. She was disappointed in me too. I could see it in her eyes even though her face smiled at me.

It is literally the only memory I can recall from that day.

Within just a few days after the wedding, I miscarried. I still remember him sitting with his mother and sobbing. I sat on the other end of the couch alone and cried because we had lost the baby, and because I was pretty sure he was crying because he thought his whole life had been ruined by me. It's not a weight I carry now. It's just the honest truth about how I felt then.

Being teenagers, we didn't make each other's lives very easy. Nearly every night I cried myself to sleep. At first it was probably from losing the baby. Then it was because I sat alone in our garage apartment after work every night while he sat with his parents in their house. After that, I think it was because I knew things were going badly and I had no sound advice from anyone with a sound mind. Some people might think I subconsciously knew what was coming, but honestly, I never saw it coming.

It had been less than five months since the wedding when his father and his father's friend showed up at the tanning salon I worked at. I couldn't make sense of why they would be at a tanning salon and then what they were trying to tell me was not right. *They were trying to trick me, but why?*

I kept asking them to repeat it because my brain couldn't comprehend the words. As they drove me to their house, they tried again to explain. I finally understood what they were saying, but I knew there was no way it could be true. It wasn't until I saw it on the evening news that it finally sank in.

The TV showed an orange truck with its hood bent into the shape of a "V," a tree standing in the middle of it. A sheet was draped over the driver's seat. He had been on his way to work when he ran off the road and hit a tree. The Arkansas State Police estimated he was going about 70 mph.

The reporter said it with such control, so matter-of-fact, with what felt like zero compassion. The news station threw it on the screen like it was just "news" and nothing to cry over. I was so mad I couldn't cry anyway.

The evening before the funeral, I was lying on my bed crying, the kind of crying that comes from a place you don't even have words for at sixteen. A friend of his family that I wasn't familiar with, walked into my room and sat down on the edge of the bed. He asked if he could pray with me, and I said yes because that's what you say in moments like that.

In his prayer, he said that God would raise him from the dead if it were His will. When he finished, I wasn't thinking about theology or doctrine, I was a scared girl who wanted her life back. So I asked him if he really thought God would do it. I needed him to tell me something solid, something hopeful, something that made sense. Instead, he told me that God would... if my faith were strong enough.

Those words would haunt my faith for many years. I stopped praying for anyone because I didn't feel like my faith was strong enough to yield any results. Mostly I prayed for myself, begging God to open a door to get me out of a situation, or let my car make it one more mile on fumes, or please just let me be invisible. I prayed the prayer of invisibility a lot.

About a week after the funeral, his mother told me I had to move out of the garage apartment attached to their house. She probably assumed I would move back in with my mom, but I was determined not to go back. Ever. I never asked my mom if I could come home, and she never offered. Instead, I set out to be the best adult I could be.

I needed a place to live so I went apartment hunting. No one asked for my drivers license and I didn't lie when I wrote my birthdate on the apartment application. The apartment manager just didn't look at it. After I'd lived there for a couple months, one afternoon while I was swimming in the pool at the apartments, she came and asked if

I was really sixteen. She said she had gotten a phone call from a lady saying that I was only sixteen and she looked at my application but was certain that I had just written down my birthdate wrong.

It could have been my mom that called her, but I really doubt it. She never tried to sway me from moving into the apartment. I think that some women at the church or some girls that I had recently offended were "concerned" and kept poking around so that anywhere I went, I couldn't get settled.

However, after telling the apartment manager that I had just gotten married, lost the baby, became a widow all within the past six months and that my mom said I couldn't come back home, she told me to keep my mouth shut and not to tell anyone how old I was and she would let me stay.

A few months later, I blew the engine up in my car because I was late for work and driving ninety miles an hour on the interstate trying to get there in a car that had no oil and no water. It was probably something a father that was a mechanic would have told me. I had a father that was a mechanic, but he had died seven years earlier. The last time I saw my father I was only about eight years old. I'm sure the thought of me driving wasn't something that was even on his radar. The step-dad that followed didn't know that he should teach me about those things. I learned that lesson the way I learned most lessons, the hard way.

Fortunately, I was able to catch a ride to work with a cousin after that. Unfortunately, that cousin, probably because he was a step-cousin, was interested in more than just giving me a ride to and from work. I was either too embarrassed to tell anyone or didn't want to risk telling anyone in case they decided that me dating him was a good idea. I knew it was a terrible idea so instead I found a job that was within walking distance.

The only problem was that I had met new friends that took advantage of my home as a place to gather and life became more about hanging out and having a good time instead of being a responsible adult. Pretty soon I was sleeping past my alarm and missing work. It didn't take long before they fired me.

I had enough money to pay my rent for the month and to buy a loaf of bread, a package of cheese and a dozen eggs, but before I could pay my rent, one of my "friends" had stolen my ATM card and my PIN which I didn't keep hidden, and withdrew my rent money from my account. When I went to withdraw the money to pay my rent, it wasn't there and the lady at the bank showed me the security footage where my "friends" had withdrawn all the money the ATM would let them have, which was everything I had left.

So I lost my apartment after about six months. One of the hardest phone calls I had to make was to my mom asking her what I should do. She said I could come back home, but I either had to work or go to school. As I was inhaling, I heard the words *"go to school"* and felt the temperature in my face rise quickly. As I was exhaling I decided to just let it go and not even start down that path. Since school was not really an option, I got a job at a local dry cleaner.

Prior to me getting pregnant, I did have a few friends that were girls, but I felt like most of them avoided me like the plague even without being pregnant. The few friends that I had in the past had all moved away and left me with no one. I quickly learned that in order to get what I thought I wanted, I could become the person I needed to be. I didn't know then that I was being exactly like my mom at that age.

The same person my mom wished that she had not been when she was my age.

When my first husband died, nothing in my life slowed down. Everything was pure chaos, and I was moving so fast I didn't have time to think, much less heal. I was running from everything I didn't know how to face, and if someone hadn't stepped in to make me stop, I probably would have jumped on a train and tried to head overseas.

And then came the comments. People kept telling me I was the youngest widow they had ever known and how that was *"just too bad,"* like I was some tragic little headline they didn't know what else to do with. But the truth was, I'd already been that sad story long before he died.

Ever since I was a little girl without a dad, the only thing anyone ever seemed to say about me was, *"Oh, how unfortunate."* That seemed to be everyone's go-to observation, the line that followed me around like a shadow. And that was not what I wanted people to think when they thought of me. I wanted them to think of me as something at least a little more glamorous.

Against her good advice, I moved out of her house and into a place where I thought I could live by my own rules, but it wasn't long before I found out that the life I thought I wanted had a price to pay that would unfold as time went on. When I have told people my story in the past, I've left out a lot of details that would incriminate me. The truth is, I made choices too that put myself in some terrible situations and I knew better when I made those choices.

In order to keep living in the nice apartment with the nice things, I had to make sure I didn't upset the person who controlled whether or not I got to stay there and that came with a whole new set of problems.

He asked me to lie and tell people I was nineteen. No one questioned it until the newspaper printed that I was seventeen when we got our marriage license. I said, "The newspaper misprints things all the time," which technically wasn't a lie. The newspaper did misprint things all the time, just not that time.

The truth is, I knew better. I knew what I was supposed to do, but I guess I thought I could bend the rules and still end up with the life I wanted. That was not the case. At seventeen, thinking I knew everything there was to know about how to live my life, that is until I found myself pregnant again and married to a high-functioning, violent alcoholic and cocaine addict. In all that confusion, I turned back to the only place I knew to get guidance: my mom.

I would have asked God, but I was furious with Him. In my mind at that time, He was the one who had wrecked my life, and I wasn't exactly eager to sit down and have a heart-to-heart. So that left me with the only person still in my life who was giving advice, even if her advice wasn't always the best.

I showed up at my mom's house with a black eye, pretending like it wasn't there and hoping she might pretend too. She didn't. She didn't ask what happened or make a scene. She just set a plate in front of me and sat down across the table, watching me the way she did when she was waiting for the truth to rise to the surface on its own.

The silence between us wasn't angry or cold. It was the kind that made it impossible to keep lying to myself. I kept my head down, picking at my food, trying to act like everything was fine even though nothing in my life had been fine for a long time.

Before I ever knew she had been diagnosed with multiple personality disorder, I tried to follow my mom's advice the best I could. I never knew if her advice came from a place of *I've been there before*, or *this is how I was raised*, or *this is what Jesus says to do*. What I did know was that on that particular day, sitting at her table with a black eye she could clearly see, I was at a complete loss for what to do. There were other bruises she couldn't see, and plenty of emotional trauma she didn't know about, but the black eye was enough.

I had a brand-new baby. By that time, I was too embarrassed to have anyone else in my life, or I had made them all mad with the stupid things I did, so I didn't have any friends. She was my only support system.

"You made your bed, now you have to lay in it."

Like I hadn't heard that line before. It was what she said every time I got caught doing something wrong.

"So, what are you going to tell people?"

I didn't talk to people. I wasn't going to tell them anything.

"Well, they're going to ask, and you'd better have an answer. They're going to talk behind your back. You look like you got hit in the eye with a baseball."

She was right. People asked. I told them I was playing tennis and got hit with a tennis ball. You could tell by the looks on their faces they didn't believe me. The sure sign was when they stopped whispering and looked away so they wouldn't have to make eye contact when I walked by.

"I can take you to a battered women's shelter. You wanted to be an adult and make adult choices, but you're not going to sleep on my couch."

I couldn't believe what I was hearing. She wanted to take me to a battered women's shelter. That was a place where I imagined other women went who had messed up their lives and didn't have a mother or anyone else to help them. They didn't know me. However, if they knew my mother they might understand. Besides, I had very little hope that they would do anything more for me than she would. The thought of it terrified me. There was no way I was going to let her drop me and my baby off at a battered women's shelter. So I told her I was going to see about getting divorced.

"You can't get divorced. Once you get married, you're married for life. You need to ask Jesus to help you."

I knew she wanted me to believe she had stayed married to my dad until he died. Years later, the memories of the girlfriend in my adult mind clued me in that he was never home unless he wanted to be home and she always begged him to come back home.

Well, right up until she suddenly didn't anymore. After she faced the shadow of death through the barrel end of a gun. That should have clued me in that they were divorced, but she would never actually tell me that she had divorced him.

I knew that she wasn't as perfect as she tried to get me to believe. My aunt told me a few stories about some of their adventures when they were teenagers. It didn't make her anything more or less in my mind than what she was, human.

I used to think my mom was of no help, but the truth was I didn't want the help she was offering because I didn't think it would get me to the place I wanted to be. I wanted the Sears catalog picture-perfect family I thought was supposed to come naturally. Leaving to go to a battered women's shelter felt like the opposite direction from where I was trying to go.

If I could have seen past my own storm, I might have noticed the one she was in. She had a baby too, just a year older than mine. Her marriage was falling apart. My teenage brother wasn't making her life easy, but his life wasn't fair or easy either. The truth was, every one of us in that family, including my step-dad, was broken in our own way. None of us knew how to say it, but we were all drowning in that brokenness just the same.

A few months later, I woke up outside on the ground. I was naked, bloody and bruised, choking on a mouthful of grass and dirt.

He had punched me in the face and the stomach. Repeatedly. He dragged me by my hair like he was some kind of caveman from one end of the house to the other.

At one point, I saw the window was open. There were people outside across the street.

I screamed for them. I screamed for anyone to please help me. It felt like my screams fell on deaf ears while I watched them walk back towards their house.

Everything went dark.

I don't remember how it started. But I know how it ended. I was tossed outside like a piece of trash.

I had no idea that it was going to keep getting worse until that very moment. Before it got to that point, I kept telling myself that kind of thing happened to everyone else and it wouldn't happen to me.

The first time I got slapped was a few hours before I was supposed to marry him. He pointed out the shirt I had just ironed still had a wrinkle. Holding it in my hands, I thought I could just iron it out real quick, but before I could even complete the thought.

His hand came across my face out of nowhere.

I thought right then *don't go through with the wedding*, but before I could say it outloud, the apologies started. And I believed them because it was easier to figure out *what am I going to do now*.

What started as a slap that would "*never happen again*" eventually turned into occasional fights, and then into a daily calculation of how to keep the truth hidden and stay alive and stay godly to the best of whatever my mom told me that was and what I believed in my heart that was. My bigger battle was trying to adjust something, my tone, my timing, my routine, my reactions, anything I thought might change the outcome of laying in the bed I had made for myself.

I buried my car keys in the dirt of a potted plant so he couldn't keep them from me.

I had to be ready at any minute. Any minute I would need to be ready to grab my keys, grab my baby and run. I always kept my purse and blankets in the car.

There were many nights we would go sleep in the parking lot of the truck stop down the street. It was especially on those mornings, I woke up doing the math. Trying to figure out what I could do differently so that night it wouldn't end the same way.

What I didn't factor in was the truth I couldn't see back then: there was absolutely nothing I could do, and nothing anyone else could do, to stop it. The violence wasn't about me, or my choices, or my mistakes. It was about him.

My next-door neighbor saw or heard what happened. She had just had surgery after being in a wreck. I know she was hurt way worse than I was — she had staples that went nearly from her head down to her feet. She helped me up and took me into her house until the police came. I filed for divorce not long after that. Of course, I filed without consulting my mom first. I told myself that if I didn't do it, my child would grow up in a worse situation than my own childhood.

He finally sobered up for good in 2018, almost thirty years later. When he finally did, he apologized. I'm sure it was part of his twelve-step program, but he was genuine and sincere. Even the things I did in retaliation, the things I carried shame for, he didn't think justified what he had done to me. Hearing that didn't erase the past, but it did tell the truth about it, and somehow that truth made it easier to let go and just let it be.

The conversation with my mom after the divorce went through was frustrating.

"Have you asked God for forgiveness?"

I was stunned. After everything that had happened to me, after everything I had survived, the first thing she wanted to know was whether I had asked God to forgive me for getting divorced.

"You know He will forgive you and allow you a divorce because you were abused."

I waited for her to ask me to wear some kind of symbol on my chest to show I was divorced and tainted. She didn't. Not that I can remember anyway.

"If I would have known, I would have told you to leave. You could have come here."

I wanted to scream, *You were going to take me to a battered women's shelter! You pretty much told me I was going to hell if I got a divorce!* But I didn't. I didn't say a lot of things to her. Partly because I wasn't confrontational, and partly because I thought maybe I was the one who had misunderstood.

Maybe I had misunderstood again. It seemed like that happened a lot. It probably felt more like months than it actually was before I spoke to her again, but I definitely didn't spend any real, quality time with her.

When I finally talked to her again, she didn't come at me with judgment or Bible verses. She told me she had put me in God's hands because she honestly believed He could take care of me better than she could. For a long time, I thought that was her way of punishing me, like she was handing me over to God because she was done trying with me.

But she wasn't being sarcastic. She never tried to be funny. She had no sense of humor at all and was always serious. She meant every word literally. In her mind, trusting God with me was the safest thing she could do.

I understand now that, in her own way, it was her personal sacrifice, giving up her need to control or manipulate me and trusting that God would take care of me for her. And in the end, it was the love of a mother who had enough faith to step out of the way and let God work it out.

Many years later, I was the chairperson of a committee selecting a project for an association of women who worked in construction-related fields. The project I chose was for the battered women's shelter. We painted and redecorated a family room so a woman and her children would have a warm, welcoming place to stay.

Even after seeing firsthand what a battered women's shelter looked like, I realized that when I was being threatened with being taken there, it had never really been the unknown that scared me. It wasn't the question of where I would sleep or what it would be like that scared me. It was the fact that I had zero hope a total stranger would want to help me or somehow make everything okay when my own mother didn't want to make it okay.

I didn't understand then that there just wasn't any way possible that she could have helped me. I was long past the days of needing a battered women's shelter, but it was only then that I could look back and see her emotional state for what it was. The mental battles she was fighting had her on the edge of a meltdown. She simply couldn't help me because she could barely hold herself together.

That moment with the iron wasn't an anomaly; it was the orientation for my new life. For the next year, I walked on eggshells, learning exactly how to make myself small so I wouldn't get crushed. The naive girl who thought she had found a savior was gone, replaced by a survivor who knew how to keep secrets.

So by the time I was eighteen, sitting in my mother's driveway, I was already an expert at hiding in plain sight.

Except for that one time she found "the pack" in the laundry basket, I had successfully hidden my smoking from her. It was never said out loud who that pack belonged to, but it didn't matter. I was tired of hiding it.

So, my barely legally an adult self sat there in the carport on a metal folding chair, a makeshift table between me and my stepdad. He was smoking. I was not, not yet, but my pack of Virginia Slims 120s was sitting right there on the table next to me, out in the open.

My mom was standing in front of me before I even knew she was there.

She had been inside with my sister, who was about to turn two, and my daughter, who had just started walking. They were having a yard sale to downsize everything they had accumulated. I had come over to help, bringing a few things of my own to sell for extra cash.

The air was thick with tension. She told me she was kicking him out. He told me he was leaving her. All I knew was that a lifetime of their prized possessions was sitting outside in the carport, priced for pennies, looking a lot less important than when they first bought them.

It was apparent that things were ending between them. Sitting there, he told me he was moving out. Then, he looked at me and asked if he could move in with me.

It was a request that would make most people cringe, but I think it was his twisted way of confessing, or perhaps an attempt at an apology. Regardless, I stopped him cold. I told him I forgave him, but I let him know in no uncertain terms that my affection for him would always be at a distance.

"You will never move in with me," I said.

It felt good to finally set things straight, to address the ordeal from years before without flinching. I made it very clear, with my words and my tone, that he was not welcome in my home. It was the second time in my short adult life that I had stood up for myself.

It was also the day my mom finally found out the truth about the cigarettes.

She looked at the table. *"Whose cigarettes are those?"*

"They're mine," I said, reaching for the pack and lighting one up.

The truth felt like fifty pounds being lifted off my shoulders.

"Oh," she said.

I knew I had disappointed her, but after that day, I never hid it from her again. I hid plenty of other things from her, things I knew would break her heart, so it felt good to give up at least one secret.

The irony, of course, was that she didn't really care about the cigarettes. She cared about whether or not I was going to grant his request. She knew he was going to ask to move in with me, and because I couldn't tell her *why* I refused him, because I didn't want to tell on him and break her heart with the truth of what he'd done, I couldn't give her a straight answer.

Because of my silence, she thought I was actually considering it and was livid about it. I know she was livid because years later, I found a journal entry where she wrote about that day.

"I am absolutely livid that she would betray me like that."

She thought I was betraying her by choosing him. The truth was, I was protecting her by keeping his secret.

They did separate and he moved out, but they never divorced. Eventually we talked about it and she believed me when I told her that I would not have betrayed her.

He got a new job, a new car and a new house. She was upset that his life was looking grand and here she was trying to follow Christ and face all the hard adult decisions you face when separating from your spouse that you share a small child with. She didn't hold back with me how she felt about him as long as my little sister wasn't around.

It wasn't too many years after he moved out that his life took a sudden devastating turn and started falling apart. Before things started getting better for him, I just didn't see how anyone could see hope in his situation and that's when my relationship with him began to heal. He became no threat to me, much less anyone else and even though I didn't do much for him, what I did do was more than someone who did nothing and I knew that he appreciated it.

He had always had one leg that was shorter than the other as a result of having a hip replacement when he was a teenager. The doctor told him that he was long overdue to have the old hip taken out and a new one put in. After he got the new hip, he got new complications.

A sore developed on his foot that wouldn't heal. He got numerous hyperbaric oxygen treatments. When it still wouldn't heal, they had to make the choice to amputate below the knee. Probably about the same time he had gotten used to the idea of having a prosthetic, they had exhausted everything they knew to do when the stump wouldn't heal. They decided to go back and amputate well above the knee.

In the middle of all that, they discovered that the hip replacement that started the whole amputation fiasco in the first place, was not a success and would have to be redone. Then, if things couldn't get worse, after the last amputation, that hip replacement was not a success and needed to be redone before it slipped and punctured a vital organ.

In the meantime, his medical leave ran out. He had to get on disability. While he was trying to get on disability, all of his money ran out. He lost his family, his job, his home, and his car, pretty much in that order. My mom wouldn't take him back. She told him to go live with his sister and he did.

Once he got on disability and had an income again, things started looking up for him. He got into a low income housing apartment for people that were disabled. It wasn't far from my mom's house and she started picking him up and taking him to church every Sunday. She told me she did it because she didn't want him to be depressed and because he was still my sister's father and it was good for him to go to church with her. Well, she did that until he must have made her mad. I never asked why she wouldn't do it anymore. I just told her I would do it. It could have been her way of getting me back in church for a few Sundays, but I honestly think she just didn't want to be around him more than she had to be.

Regardless of her reasons, I was right where I needed to be. I picked him up and took him to church several Sundays in a row. I went by and played board games, smoked cigarettes and cracked jokes with him. He wheeled around in his electric wheelchair introducing me to the friends he had made in the apartment complex. By that time, everything between me and him was forgiven and pretty much forgotten. He told me he was proud to call me his daughter. My whole life seemed better at that moment than it had in a long time.

I'll always remember the last time I saw him I had rode my new motorcycle over to his apartment so he could see it. We sat and talked about some of the good times he had with my mom and he made me laugh harder than I had laughed in a while. He told me how sorry he was about some of the rough times we had as I was growing up. As I was saying goodbye to him, I was so overwhelmed with a feeling that it was the last time I'd ever see him. On the way home I had to pull over to pull myself together and quit crying. He died the very next weekend.

CHAPTER 15

When I finally allowed myself to remember the bad memories, it opened the door to remembering the good ones too. These were memories I had unknowingly buried right alongside the painful ones. I could only do that once I understood what had been blocking them. One really big bad memory. The one I never wanted to think about. Ever. That memory was so heavy it pressed down on everything around it, smothering an entire time period of my life. It was not a fair trade, but it was the only way I knew how to cope. Even now, I know it happened, but I also have a new, better memory of that time that finally lets me breathe.

I spent years not remembering that part of my life because every time a flicker of that memory tried to cross my mind, I smothered it before it could take a full breath. I pushed it down so many times I honestly thought it was gone. And then she reminded me of it. After that, I spent the next twenty years trying to shove her memories of it away too. It took a long time for those weeds and briars of memories to turn into anything that looked like flowers.

The only way I know to explain how I finally dealt with it is this. When I stepped back and looked straight at that one really big, really bad memory and found God in it, I could finally walk down Memory

Lane without fear. I know it's hard to imagine there being any good in situations like that, but I promise you it's there. God said if I would look for Him with all my heart and soul, I would find Him. And He was right. I did find Him there.

It took those twenty something years of trying to shove the memories back into my suitcase, but when I finally found Him in the middle of it, He pulled up the weeds, roots and all, and replaced them with something better. And that's when it hit me. I wasn't just remembering a bad moment. I was remembering me, a little girl who had no idea what was happening or why. For the first time, I could see her without flinching. I could hold that memory without feeling like it was going to swallow me whole. It still hurts, but it doesn't crush me anymore. Now, when I think about being there, I don't just see the fear. I see the God who refused to leave me there.

And that is why, when she finally said she needed me to come over and talk about something she thought she remembered, I knew this was not just another conversation. It was the moment everything in her past and mine was about to collide.

When I finally did sit down with her, that's when I could hear it, the nervousness in her voice, the way her words sounded thin and unsure. She told me what she remembered.

Then she asked, *"Did it happen?"*

The words sounded echoey and far away, like they were coming from another room. I had made myself go cold, and even her question felt distant.

I wanted to be mean and sarcastic, but she only understood bluntness.

"*Yes*" was the only word I could get out. I sat there as calmly as I could and told her everything I could recall about all the nights it happened. It was like I was recalling details of a TV show I had watched, not something that had happened to me. I watched her sob and tell me how sorry she was and how she wished it had never happened. She said the worst part for her was that until this moment she had never had to think about it, but if it did happen, she knew I had been the one who had to live with that memory.

Now that I could finally look back at the little girl I used to be without falling apart, I started to see how much of my life had been shaped by trying to protect that little girl. And I had been trying to protect my mom too. Not by standing in front of her like some tiny shield, because I didn't understand danger that way yet, but in the ways a child naturally reaches for. I would crawl into my daddy's lap in the middle of one of their fights and try to pull him back into remembering I was there so he wouldn't be mad at her. In my mind, if he remembered he loved me, he would remember he loved her.

I did other things too, out-of-the-ordinary things that I know now most children wouldn't even think to do. I studied people the way other kids studied cartoons. I watched moods, tones, footsteps, the way a door closed, the way a voice changed. I pretended we weren't poor by making sure I looked like everyone else the best I could. I brushed my hair smooth, kept my clothes and shoes clean, and made sure nothing about me gave away the truth.

I took charge when Mom left us home alone, demanding my brother do exactly what I said because I didn't want her to get in trouble for leaving us there. And through all of it, I tried not to disappoint her. That was my whole world back then: protect her, protect the secrets, protect the peace, protect the image.

My daughter was still a toddler when her father's step-mother sued me for guardianship. Her father was the violent alcoholic. I had just met my boyfriend about a month before, and I thought I was doing something better for her, something steadier than the life I had been putting her through with my running around, my nights out, and the babysitters who practically raised her for a stretch. I wasn't trying to be reckless. I was just lost and trying to feel something that didn't hurt.

The truth is, I was too proud to tell anyone how bad things had gotten. I had been evicted from my apartment and had been staying in my car with my daughter for about a week. I don't even remember how I ended up moving in with him. That whole stretch of time feels like a blur of exhaustion, fear, and pretending I was fine. I only know that once we were there, it was the first time in a long time that my daughter wasn't being dragged through my chaos.

And then, right as the waves were starting to calm, my ex's step-mother hit me with a lawsuit. It felt like the ground shifted.

CHAPTER 16

I was by far not a perfect mother, but I was not a bad mother. Could I have been a better mother? *Yes*. Was I? *No*. I will admit that now. I will admit everything I did that made me a less-than-perfect mother, but I was not everything my daughter's step-grandmother made me out to be.

My mom would tell them the truth about everything, good and bad about me, but at least it would be the truth. I could live with that. I couldn't live with losing my daughter to her step-grandmother based on their false allegations and created illusions.

During the trial, they called my mom to the stand to testify. That's when their attorney pulled out the tape, holding it by the corner like it was some kind of smoking gun. My heart dropped into my stomach. He waved it in the air like it was Exhibit A in a murder trial. Staring at the tape with my head tilted to the side, I tried to read the label, and tried to understand what exactly they thought they had.

Then a thought popped in my head and before anything else happened, I leaned over to my attorney and asked if I could step out while they played it. He said it was worth asking, and he stood up and made the request.

The Judge paused everything. He agreed I didn't have to sit there and listen to it and then he turned to my mom on the stand and told her that if she consented that the voice on the recording was hers, she didn't have to listen to it either.

So we walked out of the courtroom, not in some dramatic, shoulder-to-shoulder moment, but with me feeling a very specific kind of satisfaction.

The kind money can't buy.

The kind you get from watching someone pour time, energy, and a whole lot of cash into not just trying to convince the court I was unfit and they could give my daughter a better life, but by trying to humiliate me into submission and embarrass my mom and then to force me to sit there and swallow their version of my life in the ugliest, most twisted version they could invent, and then have me fall apart on cue.

Once we were finally in the hallway, my mom looked at me with a worried expression and said, *"I remember her coming over, but I don't remember what I said."*

My mom sat beside me and apologized. I apologized too for being everything she didn't want me to be. She told me she thought what I did was honorable. That sitting in the hallway with her instead of in the courtroom took the wind right out of their sails.

It wasn't just the relationship with my daughter that was in jeopardy, the only other real relationship I had was also hanging in the balance. The one with my mom that was already barely hanging on by a thread.

The truth is, there were things they had done that were worse, and there were things I had done that were worse. I'm not ashamed of what

I've done, and I'm not proud of it either. I did what I did, and nothing can change that. But because God, my Father, has given me grace I don't deserve, I get to sleep at night. I get to live this life where I no longer walk around feeling like life with me in it was pointless.

My mom lived with more versions of herself than anyone should have to carry. I must have learned early that the only way to keep from splitting myself was to stay stoic, stay quiet, stay unnoticed. If there was a way to keep the peace, inside me or around me, that's the way I went.

My mom was trying to be a good mother, a good daughter, a good friend, a good neighbor, a good mother-in-law, a good citizen, a good church lady, and a good Christian. But she only knew how to be one of those people at a time. In a situation like that, intimidated by a wealthy, high-society woman not unlike some of the women she cleaned houses for, she would have slipped into the "good church lady/Helen's daughter" version of herself.

She would have told the truth about how she felt, not to throw me under the bus, but because she thought honesty would help me all while trying to overcome the nervousness, the panic, the anxiety of being in front of someone who made her feel small.

She was a humble housecleaner who worked for people who treated her poorly, and she still smiled and said thank you. Sincerely, because she knew that was how she got her bills paid. It took her years to learn that God would provide for her through other people and she didn't have to subject herself to mean people. I'm learning that in my own life.

She did it with far more grace than I do. I still tend to throw my sword at people from time to time. I'll hold on to it as long as I can, but if you push the right button, I'll overpower you with words I scream while standing on my tiptoes so it feels like my sword is grazing the top of your head.

I stayed in the hallway to protect myself and my mom.

She smiled at me and said, "*Thank you.*"

She told me what a good daughter I was. Words that always made me feel like *if only she knew*. She told me God was going to get me through this and everything would be okay, because everything works together for good.

There was another moment in the trial that has stayed with me, not because of what actually happened, but because of what shame can do to people. Their attorney asked me a question on the stand about something I wasn't proud of, something I had tried to forget, something I didn't want dragged into the light by someone who didn't care about the truth, only the performance of it.

I denied it.

He pressed harder.

He said he had a witness.

And then they put my babysitter, my friend, on the stand.

After she testified, I ran into her in the bathroom. She was very pregnant, mascara streaked down her face, looking like she wanted to disappear. And in that moment, I didn't feel anger or betrayal. I felt something else entirely.

I felt like we were two young women trying to survive life the best way we knew how.

And she had done what she thought she had to do.

And I had done what I thought I had to do.

And neither one of us was a villain.

Obviously, it was harder for me to admit that then, even under oath.

My mom told me later she figured they paid her to testify. I didn't blame her if they did. I probably would have taken the money too. Back then, survival didn't look noble. It looked messy. It looked like mistakes. It looked like hurting people you cared about without meaning to.

And if she ever remembers that moment and feels guilty for it, I hope she knows this:

You don't have to carry that anymore.

You don't have to punish yourself for something you did when you were young and scared and trying to survive.

You can let it go.

You can live unashamed.

Several years after my mom passed, I tried to get my hands on the tape recording. I thought I wanted to hear what she had said about me. After tracking down the court reporter and being "*this close*" to having it in my hands, I decided to leave it alone.

If I had really wanted to hear it, I should have listened to it that day in court.

It's not important to me now. What is important is that once I let go of wanting to know so badly what she said, I was finally able to start forgiving her. Once I decided in my heart that it truly did not matter, I stopped caring about whatever it was she said that day. I say things I regret all the time, most of the time it's as it's coming out of my mouth. Word vomit. Thank goodness I'm not always being recorded.

I did manage to get a copy of the attorney ad litem's report. Back then, I figured what I didn't know couldn't hurt me, which is probably why I didn't want to listen to the recording and why I don't remember seeing the report at the time either. Thirty years later, I finally had it in my hands.

The attorney ad litem was very kind to me in her report. My ex-step-mother-in-law was not. The attorney ad litem questioned her about why they would evict me and my daughter from our home, and her response was that *"she was a single mother and had to fend for herself"* and I needed to learn how to as well.

The attorney ad litem's conclusion was that their motives were not based on the welfare of my daughter, but instead demonstrated poor judgment and a vindictive character. She went on to say:

"Further, I have not found any evidence that Chris is an unfit mother. Chris impresses me as a pleasant young woman who works hard at appearing unaffected by her experiences, which others may find frustrating. She appears to be a patient, tolerant person who is bright and probably has the potential to achieve more than her circumstances have permitted thus far."

Even after the Court ruled in my favor, I maintained what I thought was a decent relationship with my daughter's step-grandmother. Anytime they asked to see her, I agreed. Well, until the day she called me at work and yelled at me because my daughter repeated a raunchy joke at her dinner table.

I didn't teach her the joke, but to be honest, I did laugh the first time I heard her repeat it. That was the truth, and that is exactly what I told her. I hung up the phone while she screamed that I was the worst mother in the world.

Apparently, when someone doesn't like you, they think a bunch of little moments of stupidity all grouped together equates to being a bad mother. It was an expensive lesson for her to learn the truth about me.

It was also one of the first of many experiences that would begin to restore my relationship with my mom.

Finding God in a really big, bad memory like that seems impossible, but over time I was able to, and I found peace there. I know what happened, and nothing can ever change that. But because I somehow managed to find God in that memory, after looking for Him over and over with all of my being, when that memory comes up now, I have a different memory alongside it. The paneled walls in the room, the smell of rain, the sound of thunder, the feel of the wind blowing through the open window and watching the blue curtain above my head twist and turn and flutter. She came into the room and I was not scared anymore.

It turns out that I'm still not proud of all the choices I made while trying to navigate a life that was hard not just from my own making, but I am not ashamed anymore. Life has left me with a few more scars than I had then, but I'm hoping one day people will see me as that *"patient, tolerant person"* again who *"has the potential to achieve more than her circumstances have permitted thus far."*

CHAPTER 17

Not long after the trial ended, right before I enrolled in community college, life shifted back into something that almost looked normal. Me and my girls drove to Alabama and met my mom and the rest of the family to spend Thanksgiving with my grandparents.

My Grandma Jackie had been in my life so long that I didn't even know she was technically a "step" until I was a teenager. She was just Grandma Jackie. And that Thanksgiving, Grandma Jackie told me she could put highlights in my hair.

I had never colored my hair. I barely even went to get it cut. That was a luxury I couldn't afford, so when she offered to highlight it, I didn't stop to question her ability. I probably should have.

Needless to say, it did not turn out the way I expected it to. I'm not super picky about what I get when I ask for something, at least I try not to be, but what happened to my hair was unlike anything I could have imagined. I still don't know how she managed it. When she took the foil out and I went to wash the chemicals out in the shower, I was not prepared for what I saw.

I dried my hair with a towel and looked in the mirror. I was mortified.

Huge blonde polka dots.

All over my brunette hair.

Huge polka dots.

All I could do was dry my tears and tell myself to hold it together until I got in the car to drive home. My grandmother would have been crushed if she knew how upset I was. When I finally walked out of the bathroom, she said it looked beautiful. Everyone else said it was beautiful too, even though their eyes said something completely different. Their eyes were big with surprise, and not the good kind of surprise.

When I finally made it onto the highway and my girls fell asleep in the backseat, I cried until I had no tears left.

When I got home, I tried dyeing it blonde. That was a mistake. My hair turned the color of a bright red fire truck. So I took the risk of all my hair falling out and went to Walmart wearing a baseball cap to buy dark brown hair color. It ended up turning a weird shade of orange, but at least I wasn't polka dotted anymore.

So when I showed up at the community college office, my hair was still orange. Not a fashion statement, just the aftermath of trying to fix the polka-dot disaster myself. At that point in my life, if something wasn't going to hurt my circumstances and it cost money to fix, it went straight to the bottom of the priority list. I just wanted to make something better of myself. From what I could tell, all the church kids who somehow missed the fallout of high school pregnancy and addiction had gone to college, and if you were in the income class I was in, community college seemed like a fair trade.

The college didn't recognize my homeschooling education and told me that if I wanted to attend, I would have to get my GED. My mom told me she had never graduated high school and had dropped out in the eighth grade. Now she wanted to get her GED too. I keep thinking that surely I must have realized what a big deal that was for her. But the memories I want to recall won't come back. I don't remember studying with her. I don't remember taking the tests with her.

I do remember that we both took the GED test. And we both passed.

I don't remember exactly when or why, but somehow I ended up on the phone with a lady asking me to give a speech at the state GED graduation. A speech. In front of a crowd. On a stage. I didn't even think to ask if not getting up there was an option.

So my immature self came up with a solution on the fly. Before I could stop myself, the words *"Can I sing instead?"* came out of my mouth. I couldn't speak in front of people, but I could sing if I absolutely had to.

I was so excited that my mom's decision to homeschool me wasn't going to keep me from experiencing a tiny piece of what it must have felt like to graduate with a class. There was no way I was going to let anyone, not even me, mess that up.

The memory I have of that day is that my mom didn't know how I really felt. I couldn't see her in the crowd, so for all I know she might've been crying, or she might not have been. I don't even know if I wanted her to be crying. Maybe I did. What I do remember is standing there singing *Wind Beneath My Wings* and I even threw in *"for my mom who is graduating with me today,"* and trying to make it sound like something I actually believed.

I have no doubt she was proud of me at times. When I visited her during the holidays, she didn't tell me how ashamed she was of me. She saved those conversations for another time, usually over the phone or written into journals I never got to see. The holidays were the one place she seemed to set all of that aside. She let herself enjoy me, and she let me enjoy her. It was like we both silently agreed to call a truce, no criticism, no disappointment, no reminders of who I wasn't measuring up to be. Just mother and daughter pretending, for a little while, that we weren't carrying everything we carried the rest of the year.

Life didn't slow down after that. It never did back then. One moment I was standing on a stage singing for my mom, and the next I was being pulled into something heavier, something I didn't see coming.

I had just left the day before to come back home from visiting my grandfather in the hospital in Alabama. I was at work when the receptionist came to find me and said I had an important phone call. It was one of the nurses from the hospital. She told me she couldn't find my Grandma Jackie and was sorry she had to call me, but my grandfather was about to pass. It mattered to her that he didn't leave this world alone.

My grandfather and my grandmother eventually divorced, and he married my "Grandma Jackie." I don't remember a time when she wasn't around. I didn't think of her as a step-anything. Truth be told, she was probably my favorite of all my grandparents. Maybe because I don't remember her ever saying she hated anyone in our family. That alone set her apart.

My first memory of my grandfather was when he and Grandma Jackie lived in Onalaska, Texas, on Lake Livingston. He roofed boat docks, cut glass, did woodworking, and sewed. I don't know why it fascinated me, but my most vivid memory of the two of them is watching them make quilts together. He was so proud of the wooden patterns he made for cutting out the quilt blocks. I watched him sew the blocks together, and then the two of them worked side by side on the hand stitching. When I was nine years old, he found an old sewing machine in a dumpster and refurbished it for me. I sewed on that thing until the gears fell off.

They eventually moved to Brilliant, Alabama, to be closer to her family. It didn't matter to me where they lived, they still came to visit us at least once a year. Funny thing now is, I didn't pay enough attention to notice how their visits affected my mom. I was too wrapped up in playing games with my grandparents or learning to sew.

The nurse held the phone up to my grandfather's ear so I could talk to him, so he would know he wasn't alone. I don't remember everything I said, but I know I told him how much I loved him and that I was sorry that it was my voice he would hear last. I heard him take his final breath, and the nurse told me he was gone.

The one thing I regret is telling him I was sorry. I wasn't sorry. My voice was the last voice he ever heard, and because of that, I feel honored. not sorry.

The funeral was on July 20, 2000. By then, I was pretty good at recognizing when my mom was about to switch to a different personality. It was the first time she had seen her brothers and sister in a while, and she was nervous. We had a plan to try to keep her in the moment. We both carried recent pictures of my girls and my nephew, and I had a set of questions ready to ask her. We had never tried it before, but I hoped it would work.

I only had to use the questions once, and we were alone when it happened. We had just crossed over the Alabama state line. She had started telling me a story about my dad and my grandfather when she took a long, awkward pause.

"Mom, you okay?"

She stared straight ahead, blank.

"Mom?"

"There are some stories about my life that are just too hard to tell."

It was Gertrude. That's the name I gave her. She was such a prude and probably irritated me more than any of the other personalities. I couldn't stand her. And now here I was, stuck in the car with her and she was standing between me and something I treasured but rarely got: a story about my dad.

"Mom, who am I?"

"You are my dear, sweet daughter."

"What year is it?"

"It's the year of our Lord."

"Who are your grandkids? Mom, look at the pictures. Mom, it's okay. Don't cry. It was just for a minute and you're back. I'll start with showing you the pictures first next time."

There were so many things about my mom's life that didn't make sense to me for years. Her therapist tried to explain it, but even he didn't understand the depth of what she was carrying. Honestly, neither did I. Not until much later, when I started having episodes of the same kind she had tried to describe. Suddenly her fear, her confusion, her constant self-doubt, all of it came into focus. And I thought *if I had known then what I know now, I could have loved her better.*

People like to call it mental illness, but that word never fit her. She wasn't broken. She wasn't weak. She was a woman who had endured more mental strain than any one person should ever have to hold, and eventually something inside her cracked under the weight. That's not illness. That's a human being pushed past her limits. And when someone reaches that point, it doesn't mean they need to be fixed. It means they need to be loved even more intentionally, more gently, more consistently than ever.

This is where God steps in. He fills the cracks we can't reach. He does it in ways we don't always see, and He does it through people who show up with compassion instead of judgment. I didn't know how to offer that kind of love back then. But when I look at her journals now, I see a woman who was trying so hard to stay good, to stay in control, to keep from sinning, even as the world around her kept knocking her off balance.

And when I read the entry about her dad burning that box of paper projects, I finally understood the kind of wound she was living with. A little girl who believed she had sinned because someone else destroyed something precious to her. A little girl who learned to carry guilt that never belonged to her. A little girl who grew into a woman still trying to keep promises she was never allowed to keep.

I didn't understand the weight she carried every day until I read this journal entry dated August 9, 1994.

> **"Last time I wrote about a time when my Dad had burned up a box of paper projects my teacher had given me. I felt angry last week I guess because of his inability to sense how important that**

box of papers was to me. I remember something else. Because this happened I was sure I must be wrong. I must have been coveting or lusting that's why it happened. I think this is still stuck in my head, but at least I see it now.

Also something else went in my head. This particular time we were moving it was right after the school year had ended. I guess this teacher was cleaning out her closet or something because she came across this box of paper projects. She said she would give them to me if I would promise to do them.

They were cut out and make something papers, and of course I promised.

The importance of promise keeping was at that time great in my life. I knew you were to keep your promises. The fact to me was if you didn't you were real bad. But what were you if someone else interfered beyond your control, to make you sin. Still bad right!? This is really an important issue.

It just happens I have boxes of paper projects to be done with children. I've been saving them, even though it's not exactly the same I see

similarities. And I see my trying to stay in control so I won't sin. I won't be made to sin.

Yet in my efforts to control I've led a defeated life.

Somehow always someone or something keeps me from fulfilling my mission.

I'm just about to pick it up and try it again. Doing the projects with another child or children in place of me doing them myself.

And because of the distraction and problems I feel again as though I'm sinning. I'm still not able to keep my promise to my teacher.

Diane Beadle – August 9, 1994

Reading her words, I could see the little girl still trapped inside the woman I called Mom, trying to make sense of pain she never should have had to carry. She wasn't crazy. She wasn't weak. She was wounded. The world had taught her to blame herself for every crack someone else put in her.

What I know now is that God never looked at her the way she looked at herself. He wasn't keeping score. He wasn't waiting for her to get it right. He was trying to hold together the pieces of a heart that had been breaking since childhood. And if anyone needed the kind of love that fills in the gaps and steadies the ground under your feet, it was her.

I didn't understand any of that back then. Not until the day she called me and told me her diagnosis. That was the moment everything shifted, even though I didn't realize it at the time.

CHAPTER 18

I pulled into the grocery store parking lot like she asked. I didn't think anything of it. She had a way of sounding serious even when she was just asking what I was cooking for dinner, so I wasn't bracing for anything life-altering. I was just trying to breathe through another day of a marriage that felt like walking barefoot on broken glass.

"Okay, I'm parked. What is it?"

She didn't ease into it. She never did. She went straight for the center of the target.

"I've been having some problems with my memory, so I went to see a therapist."

That didn't surprise me. She had always been forgetful in ways that didn't make sense. Whole conversations missing. Whole days missing. Whole versions of herself missing. I had confronted her about it before, but she always brushed it off like I was imagining things.

"And what did the therapist tell you?"

"He said I'm having trouble being the real me."

I could have told her that. I had told her that. But hearing her say it out loud, hearing her admit it, hearing her voice shake just a little. That was new.

Then she said it.

"He thinks I may have multiple personality disorder."

She said it like a sentence being handed down. Like a verdict. Like the end of her credibility, her dignity, her voice. She wasn't afraid of the diagnosis. She was afraid of being dismissed. She was afraid no one would ever believe her again.

And all I could think was, *God, help her. Help me help her.*

I didn't gasp. I didn't argue. I didn't tell her she was wrong. I didn't tell her she was right. I just sat there in my car, staring at the steering wheel, feeling the weight of something I didn't understand yet.

The only reference point I had was a movie. *Sybil*. The dramatic, over-the-top Hollywood version. My mom and I had watched it together years earlier, and she didn't even remember that. She didn't remember the popcorn, the pauses, the way I sat there glued to the screen. She didn't remember any of it.

"Like Sybil?" I asked.

"Who is Sybil?"

"The movie, Mom."

"I don't know what you're talking about."

And that was the moment something inside me shifted. Because every detail of that movie suddenly flooded my head. She remembered none of it. And suddenly the diagnosis didn't feel dramatic at all. It felt real. It felt familiar. It felt like something I had been living with my whole life without having a name for it.

"So how many of these things do you have?"

"We don't know yet. At least six."

Six. At least. She said it like she was telling me the weather. Like she had already accepted that this was her new identity. Like she was preparing herself for me to walk away.

I didn't walk away. But I did hang up the phone and fall straight into the place I always went when life got too big, deep thought. The kind of deep thought that swallows you whole. The kind that makes the world go quiet. The kind my kids eventually learned to pull me out of by saying "*Mom*" ten times in a row.

I didn't tell anyone. Not a soul. I covered for her. I protected her. I prayed for her. I argued with God about her. And then I tried to figure out how to live with a mother whose mind had been pushed past its limits long before anyone ever gave it a name.

I didn't call her back for a while after that. Not because I didn't love her, but because I didn't know what to do with what she had just told me. I didn't have a category for it. I didn't have the tools. I didn't have the maturity. I didn't have the faith I have now. All I had was a head full of questions and a heart that didn't know where to put them.

I was angry. Not at her. At the situation. At the unfairness of it. At the fact that she had lived through so much trauma that her mind had to split itself into pieces just to survive. At the fact that she thought this diagnosis meant she was unworthy of being believed. At the fact that she thought she was alone.

I didn't know how to tell her any of that. So I didn't. I stayed quiet. She stayed quiet. And the silence between us grew thick enough to feel like a wall. She assumed I wanted nothing more to do with her. She wasn't wrong. At the time, I didn't. I needed space to breathe. I needed space to think. I needed space to figure out how to love a mother whose mind had been pushed past its limits long before I ever came along.

It took her weeks to call me again. Not because she didn't want to, but because she didn't want to force herself into my life if I didn't want her there. She tiptoed around my silence like she was afraid of breaking something fragile. She didn't realize I was the one who felt fragile.

That was also the season when I learned something that shaped the rest of my life: if you have no expectations, you can't be disappointed. I took that lesson too far, and it cost me in ways I didn't understand until much later. But at the time, it felt like survival. Eventually I came back around. I always did. And when I did, I started trying to figure out her personalities. Not because I thought it was interesting, but because I needed to know who I was talking to. I needed to know how to respond. I needed to know how to protect myself and her at the same time.

It didn't take long to realize there were more than six. She was like Arkansas weather. If I didn't like the one I was dealing with, I could wait fifteen minutes and she'd change. You can laugh. I do now. But back then, it was exhausting. Confusing. Sometimes terrifying. And sometimes strangely comforting, because at least one of them usually liked me.

When I started reading her journals, I started seeing the world through her eyes.

That was when I realized she wasn't a diagnosis.

She was a woman who had been fighting for her sanity since childhood. That was when everything began to make sense. Some of the pages were written by her as Diane. But many weren't. Some were written by the little girl inside her. Some were written by the protector. Some were written by the one who carried the shame. Some were written by the one who carried the anger. Some were written by the one who carried the memories she couldn't bear to hold.

There were drawings. Paintings. Letters. Conversations between her and the parts of herself she didn't understand. Questions she asked her alters. Answers they wrote back. It was like watching her mind try to negotiate with itself.

One letter was from an alter named Carrol. The handwriting looked like it belonged to an eight-year-old. The words did too.

"When I feel like you are not so afraid I can talk better. My name is Carrol. When you hear me talk I'm not hurting. I just need your attention. But you are so afraid. Only babies are."

And then my mom wrote back to her.

"Thank you Carrol for sharing. I can let you come with me today, but not drive. Please stay in your safe place while I drive."

I read that and thought, *Lord, she was driving around as an eight-year-old.* No wonder she didn't drive well. The more I read, the more I realized how hard her life had been. She questioned every step she made. Every decision. Every conversation. She prayed about everything. What she ate. What time she ate it. Who she talked to. What she said. Whether she was sinning. Whether she was disappointing God. Whether she was disappointing herself.

I used to tell her, "Mom, just follow your heart and stop stressing about every move you make." I had no idea how impossible that really was for her. Her journals were full of letters to God. Pages and pages of her trying to figure out His will. Trying to stay in control. Trying not to sin. Trying not to break. Trying to be good enough for a God who never asked her to earn His love.

One letter asked God if it would be okay to save five dollars a week for a dishwasher. She told Him she would save for fifty weeks, and if He didn't answer by then, she would keep washing dishes by hand.

She even wondered if she should teach my little sister to wash dishes because it would build character. Then she wrote that she was a bad person for wanting to give her child a chore she hated.

That was my mom. Trying to be perfect. Trying to be holy. Trying to be enough. Trying to keep promises she was never allowed to keep.

One of the earliest journal entries I found was dated April 4, 1991.

> "I'm reading *End of False Guilt*, a paragraph a day on tape. And meditating or bringing back to remember during the day what has been said. Listened to tape by Craig Landfair on Rethink First Love. Scripture booklet has to do with that which is not of faith can't please God. Well, that was the scripture I meditated on. Booklet's scripture was Romans 14:23 part B: 'and whatever is not from faith is sin.'
>
> Awoke with a vision of a fire just about to go out and as I asked the Lord for scriptures to think on today the fire was built back up again.
>
> May it so be the love in my heart for Thee, my dear Lord."
>
> Diane Beadle – April 4, 1991

Her birth certificate spelled her name with two N's, but she never used them. She always wrote Diane. Maybe it was a small way of separating herself from the girl she used to be. I didn't even know the "official" spelling until the funeral home asked me to double check.

For years I carried resentment over the fact that she named me Chris. Before we moved away from England, Arkansas, everyone called me Sissy. My dad's family. My mom's family. All of them. After we moved to Little Rock, the nickname vanished and I became Chris again, like that softer version of me had been left behind with the rest of our old life.

Life with her was never predictable. I could count on being fed, clothed, and sheltered, but affection was something she kept at a distance. Loving her felt complicated, and loving me seemed even harder for her. Maybe she didn't grow up with affection. Maybe she was afraid of slipping back into old patterns. Maybe she simply didn't know how to let love in without feeling like she was doing something wrong.

At one point she apologized for the way she had treated me. She said hurting me was like shooting an arrow into my heart and then yanking it back out. The wound would eventually scar, and that scar would keep the next arrow from sinking in so deep. She believed she was toughening me up for the world. In reality, she was teaching me to build walls.

Those walls went up early. Every time I reached for her and she pushed me away or dismissed my affection as obligation, another layer of protection formed. She must have told me she loved me at some point, but I don't remember hearing the words until I was in my thirties. By then she had softened. She hugged me tight every time she saw me. She said the words out loud. She even admitted she was trying to make up for all the hugs she withheld when I was little.

She understood the damage she had done. I lived inside a prison built from scars and self-protection. Blaming her for putting me there didn't help, and blaming myself for reinforcing the walls didn't either. She probably never imagined how those scars would shape my life. Yet she also gave me the key to get out. She told me the only way to heal the scars was to receive love, and the only way to bring down the walls was to trust. Two things she struggled with her entire life.

Maybe she locked me in that prison, but she also left a way out. I found it in a journal entry written from a softer place in her heart, a place she never showed me face-to-face. Reading it felt like hearing her ask for forgiveness in the only way she knew how.

The journal entry I found next was dated April 19, 1995. It was titled *Prayer for Chris.*

> "A good place to realize you judge others is how you judge Chris. She is stoic and in control of her feelings around you. Unable to express her feelings to you or her children. Unable to see that what she judges you for she herself is guilty of. However, you see yourself being judgmental. However, the judging benefits no one. Not Chris. Not her children. Lord, please help me give Chris some grace. Yet my faith is so weak. My hope is weaker still. And my love. Who knows if it's there at all?
>
> Morning prayer. Heavenly Father please forgive Chris for not knowing her feelings today. Please help her receive love from you and give love to others. Please

forgive her rebellion that resists ways and plans that would break the stoic emotions and give her freedom from her prison. Please set her free from the lies she has believed that say to love not at all is a safe way to keep yourself from hurt. Please open for her a treasure chest of warmth and love.

The longing in my young daughter's soul makes me ache to see. I know what it is. She simply wants to take care of me. Did I do that? I do not know. Maybe she was obsessed from birth. To feel as though taking care of someone will really give self-worth. How does someone wake her up to see. That is not it indeed. Your worth my dear has already been given as if by decree.

You are beautiful. You are lovely. You are awesome and you are of great worth. You are valuable. You are smart. You are who you are. You do not have to please someone to be okay.

And give her hope that she is above all loved. Her being abandoned was a lie. Her being unwanted was a lie. Her needs should not be met was a lie. She is important. She is a jewel. She can feel and live and survive.

Help her feel Lord. Please help her feel. Please help me

see Your unjudging grace given to her. Please help me feel Your forgiveness and grace as it is released to her.

For You Lord do not judge the stoic. You do not judge the unforgiving or the hard in heart today. Your day of judgment has not come. Release us Lord to accept Your day as You have announced it to be.

Help us to receive it.

It's called grace.

This is Your day of grace.

In Jesus' name I pray.

Amen.

Diane Beadle, 4-19-95"

My life has been a reflection of every word she prayed. I never could do those two things together, receive love and trust. When I read this entry for the first time, I sat there stunned by the irony. She wrote it thirty years earlier while sitting in her own prison, and there I was, decades later, sitting in mine. Yet she loved me enough back then to leave a note I would find at the exact moment I needed it, telling me I didn't have to stay locked up anymore. It felt almost prophetic, as if she knew the "prison" she lived in would be passed down to me.

If she taught me anything of lasting value, it was to believe in God. Her doctrine wasn't always right, she had been taught things that twisted her understanding, but the core of her faith was simple: trust God personally. When I lost my way, all I had to do was ask Him for help, and He always showed me a way out.

I just didn't always take it. Most of my life I chose the easier path, the one that led straight into my own personal hell.

She tried to teach me the difference between living in the world and not being of it, but because she lied about her past, none of it made sense. I understood the words, but I didn't have the life experience to understand the meaning. What was supposed to scare me at twelve years old only intrigued me. After all, she had done everything she warned me not to do, and she seemed fine or so I thought.

She told me smoking was bad, yet my step-dad smoked in our house. She told me premarital sex was wrong, and I caught her doing it. She told me drugs were dangerous, then admitted she wished she had never taken LSD when she was pregnant.

Following my heart brought moments of happiness, but they never lasted. Eventually I realized what she had been trying to tell me: the foundation you build your life on determines everything you chase after. I chased after people, people I hoped would love me, protect me, want the same things I wanted. Those same people who ended up breaking me.

When we lived in that rundown trailer with holes in the floor, my mom cut out a picture of a little white house and taped it to the refrigerator. Not long after, we had that little white house.

I sat on my bedroom floor in that little white house with the Sears catalog, cutting out pictures of the models who looked like the perfect family. I carefully cut out pictures of the life I wanted. I cut out the pristine living room sets, the manicured lawns, the happy families gathering around dining tables that didn't have scratches on them. I pasted them into scrapbooks, building a paper world where everything was safe, beautiful, and "normal."

I knew better than to tape my perfect family to the fridge, so I kept it hidden and dreamed of escaping the chaos I didn't think I belonged in.

And now, nearly thirty years later, I was living inside the scrapbook. I thought I had finally made it.

On the surface, I had everything I had ever cut out of those pages. The house. The cars. The appearance of a stable, successful life. If you looked at me from the street, or on Facebook, I was the picture of the American Dream.

But pictures are flat, and so was my life.

The reality was a slow, quiet suffocation. I realized too late that I wasn't a partner in this life. I was a prop. I was working myself into the ground for someone else's enjoyment, maintaining the set design for a play where I didn't have a speaking role. I had all the "stuff" anyone could want, but I was lonelier in that beautiful house than I had ever been in my whole life.

I had chased the picture-perfect dream, only to find out that the people in those pictures aren't real. Every time someone I followed after left or turned on me, my spirit shattered a little more.

But when God became my foundation, everything changed. I stopped letting people in who didn't want what He wanted for me. I started living like someone who belonged to Him. Even when everything around me fell apart, I stayed standing because He was the ground under my feet.

Eventually I realized it was His idea all along to give me to my mom. I'm sure He already told her I told you so. Once I accepted that, some forty years later, His word finally started making sense.

I spent decades learning what love was not. It took years more to learn what love actually is. Healing came slowly, one small act of trust at a time. I started with something simple, trusting the sun to rise. Every morning I watched it come up. Every evening I watched it go down. That rhythm softened me. It taught me to trust again. And eventually, the walls I had built began to crumble.

Today I can love with a raw, fierce love that lived behind those walls for years. My mom eventually found her own freedom too. But before she did, she wrote this:

> "The captive you see has no name.
> She's been placed in this cage.
> She accepts the blame.
> Though pushed and shoved it's plain to see
> that Helen's daughter could only be
> what she is today to accept what she could.
> The affirmation she must be good
> and others just never did hardly see
> that Helen's daughter's heart really bleeds.
> It bleeds when broken.
> It bleeds when bruised.
> She's been abused.
> For fear the whole world would really find out,

Helen's daughter could only pout.
And away she went into her cage.
Away she went instead of letting the rage
that had built up within her really come out.
She just went and sulked and barely pouted.
Well one day someone said,
'Why do you care about what that woman says?'
and so you pout.
Helen's daughter has never been anything except that
you see.
She wants to be given a name.
But the one who named her is insane.
So how can she leave her cage where she lives?
How can she go and explore how to live?
It's Helen's daughter who still lives there.
But today she says I must declare
Independence from that awful fate.
And say though I'm nameless I can only wait
til the one I belong to comes and takes me away.
And she thought just why do I care?
Why do I let her keep me here?
Why don't I just say hey so what.
If you don't like me I don't care.
It doesn't matter, I really don't care.
I really think I'll get out of here.
So why don't I leave.
Why don't I go?
There isn't an answer to give my heart hope.

I just continue to look through the bars
even though the cage's door is open.
I just can't go.
Then His name on my head I'll bear.
Out I come into the sun.
Out I come I'll surely run.
Helen's daughter is not here.
Danielle."
Diane Beadle – *Helen's Daughter*

Pretending things didn't hurt became second nature to me. I learned early on to swallow pain before it could settle, to shut down feelings before they had a chance to form. Over time, that habit didn't just numb my own emotions, it dulled my understanding of Christ's suffering too. I knew the story. I knew the cross. I knew the words. But I couldn't feel any of it. Not in a way that reached my heart.

When you harden yourself to survive, even the love of God hits like rain on stone. I could acknowledge what Jesus endured, but the weight of it never landed. The emotional agony He carried. The physical torment. The loneliness, betrayal, and abandonment, all of it meant for my healing, yet I stayed disconnected because I had trained myself not to feel anything deeply.

Walls don't just keep hurt out. They keep revelation out too.

For years I assumed His suffering was meant to spare me from feeling mine. That wasn't the point at all. What He endured was meant to show me that He understood every kind of pain I carried no matter how it happened or who caused it. He wanted to enter the places I had buried and the memories I avoided. He understood those wounds in a way no one else ever could.

I minimized His suffering the same way I minimized my own. Both became distant facts instead of intimate truths. It took a long time to realize the cross wasn't just about salvation. It was about a God who stepped into the very kind of pain I kept running from and felt every ounce of it on purpose. He entered the hidden places, the ones I didn't want to look at, the ones I didn't think were worth tending.

Those walls I built didn't just keep people out. They kept Him out too. And I didn't even realize it. Looking back now, I can see how all of it, the walls, the numbness, the confusion, the distance between my mom and me, even the silence I kept with God, was part of a much longer story I didn't know I was living. I thought I was surviving one moment at a time, but something deeper was happening beneath the surface. God was already working His way into the places I had locked up tight, and my mom, in her own broken and beautiful way, was leaving me breadcrumbs to follow long after she was gone. I didn't understand any of it then. I only knew that something in me was shifting, and the next chapter of my life was about to expose things I had spent years trying not to remember.

CHAPTER 19

Her life wasn't easy. Balance never came naturally to her, so she created her own version of it. The only way she knew to keep herself steady was to live a certain way, and part of that meant staying single. After she separated from my stepdad, she tried to stay friends with him. They never divorced. If he was sick, she took him food. If he needed medicine, she picked it up. She didn't do it because he deserved it. She did it because she believed Jesus would have done it for him. Once she no longer felt responsible for him, she stopped trying to make him like her. Her choices weren't based on his behavior. They were based on her faith.

Whenever I complained about my own struggles, she reminded me that I shouldn't be living the lifestyle I was living. Back then, I thought she was embarrassed of me. She cleaned houses for wealthy families who looked perfect from the outside, and I assumed she wanted us to at least pretend to be like them. Now I know she wasn't thinking about appearances at all. She believed that if I were married instead of cohabitating, I would be more aligned with God's will. And if I were aligned with God's will, then the man I lived with would be held accountable by God Himself. In her mind, he would either treat me the way a wife should be treated, or he would face God's correction. That was her logic.

Part of me wanted to say, if you only knew them, you wouldn't be pushing me so hard. But I got tired of hearing about how I was living in sin every time we talked. It became easier to lie about someone living with me than to listen to the lecture. Eventually the lie got too heavy to carry, and I stopped trying to keep it going.

She didn't agree with a single thing I was doing. She hated the smoking, the rebellion, and the chaos I was inviting in. But by the time I was in my thirties, something shifted. She stopped trying to fix me and started just loving me.

I would sit at her table, and even though I knew she wished I was living differently, she quit making me feel like I didn't belong there with her. She finally accepted me as I was, not as who she wanted me to be. In a weird twist of fate, the woman who used to terrify me with her judgment became the only person in the world who made me feel safe enough to just be Chris.

By then, I finally decided to quit lying to her altogether. I knew she felt a twinge in her spirit every time I lied, and she always gave me a chance to tell the truth. I just couldn't do it. Her expectations of me were simple: be good. If I was good, people would say, *"What a perfect little girl you have."* But the life I lived behind the lie was nothing close to the version she wanted to believe. She told me that once herself.

"I have nothing good I can say about you to anyone because you are so far from the Lord, there is nothing good there. I'm not even sure that Jesus will allow me to claim you as my daughter."

It sounds harsh, but she wasn't trying to hurt me. She was telling the truth as she saw it. And the truth was, I had been living a double life for years. I was the girl who wrote a monthly Christian newsletter for my community and started a prayer group that included my mom and her friends. I was also the girl who would go off the deep end and get sucked right back into the world the moment life got too heavy. My relationship with God was on again, off again. I wanted the appearance of surrender without the cost of it. I wanted my mom to think I was living for Christ, even when I wasn't.

Looking back, I have compassion for that version of myself. I wasn't always purposely trying to be rebellious. I was trying to balance everything. I was trying to keep my kids safe, keep my relationships from falling apart, keep my own emptiness from swallowing me whole. I wanted peace, even if I had to lie to get it. I wanted a mother who could tell me how to do life better than I was doing it, but also accept that I wasn't ready to live fully surrendered to Christ. I wanted her approval without wanting her lifestyle.

Instead, I spiraled. I went places I never thought I'd go. I realized I might have gone too far when I found myself worried about the Hells Angels becoming involved in my life. Around that same time, my nineteen-year-old daughter walked in on me sitting in my living room, passing around a joint wrapped in rebel flag paper.

I asked her if she wanted to hit it. That was the only thing I could think to say that wouldn't embarrass anyone or make the moment more awkward. Except it embarrassed me. My insides cringed at the person I had become, someone who thought offering her child a joint was somehow the cool thing to do. I knew I had to be better than that.

My daughter and I have talked about that day, and others like it. We've talked about the drugs, but also the anger. She told me once that when she and her husband argue, she sometimes wants to argue back. But then she looks at my granddaughter and remembers the arguments she witnessed as a child. She takes a deep breath and walks away so her daughter won't experience the emotional trauma she could prevent. Trauma I could have prevented. Trauma she somehow made peace with because she knows her daughter will never go through that with her.

My mom didn't see the whole picture, but she didn't need to. She was right. I kept that part of my life hidden, but she knew something was off. It's almost impossible not to imitate the company you keep. Even if I didn't look like them, my values, my morals, and my opinions had shifted.

Eventually I stopped trying to be the daughter she wanted and decided to be myself instead of the version I thought she expected. All I could do was live the best way I knew how and hope she would still accept me. Some things in my life needed to change, and I knew it. When she questioned me, I told her, "Sometimes the visual results of repentance don't happen overnight."

It was like a light came on for both of us. From that day forward, our relationship started to heal. Slowly, steadily, almost quietly. A seed had been planted, and depending on how we cared for it, it would either grow stronger or begin to wilt. We chose to tend it.

I didn't know it then, but that season was the beginning of God pulling me back toward Himself, even while I was still running in the opposite direction. My life was unraveling in ways I couldn't control, yet somehow He kept threading grace through every loose end. My mom and I were both learning how to love each other from the places we were, not the places we wished we could be. Something in me was shifting, something in her was softening, and for the first time in a long time, I felt the faintest hint of hope that neither of us would stay the same.

Chapter 20

After she died, my spiritual life rose and fell like the tide. Some seasons I felt close to God, and other seasons I drifted so far I could barely see the shoreline. I learned the hard way, as I usually do, that my life only began to steady itself when I slowly brought my values and morals back into alignment with the kind of life God had been calling me to live all along. It's taken me years, but God still waited, just like He waited for Noah.

I've told you a lot about the things my mom struggled with, the things she didn't always get right, but it's only fair to tell you what she did do right.

She never cared who was watching her worship. She never toned it down or made it palatable for anyone else's comfort. Sometimes I would lie beside her and listen to her speak in tongues for what felt like hours. I rested my head in her lap while she prayed. That sound of her voice is etched into me. It was the first place I ever felt the presence of God, even if I didn't understand it at the time.

From the very beginning of my life, I listened to that same sound of her voice vibrating through her chest while I looked up at her face and watched her eyelashes fluttering like she was forcing her eyelids to stay closed.

As I got older, other kids tried to convince me I should be embarrassed of her. She didn't look anything like the mom I had cut out of the Sears catalog. It took me years to realize the reason I never taped that picture-perfect family to the fridge was because deep down, I didn't actually want them. I wanted the mom God gave me. The one I was blessed with. I just didn't believe it sometimes.

Whenever it felt like my world was falling apart, she reminded me that I was loved by God whose love I could never outrun. A Father who loved me and her no matter what we did, no matter how far we wandered, no matter how many times we had to start over.

Looking back over just the past three years of my life, I can see the places where God swooped in and caught me. I can see where He put me back together again. I can see where He gave me more than my heart ever knew how to ask for. Somewhere along the way, I lost my taste for certain things. My priorities shifted. My perspective changed. And all of that part happened so quietly that I didn't even realize I was being rebuilt until I looked back and saw the difference.

What was literally happening to make that change didn't come through a quiet meditation or a peaceful realization. It came through a cup of coffee and a face-plant on a tile floor.

If the 100k was the moment I realized I was living an illusion, 2024 was the year God finally stripped the stage lights away. I thought I was training for a 100-mile race, but He was training me to finally stop running altogether.

Starting out with Eric was easy. We shared a world, a circle of friends, and a pace that felt natural. But then the physical part of me broke. I reached for a spilled cup of coffee and my back just gave up.

In an instant, I wasn't a runner anymore. I was just someone trying to navigate a body that felt like it had betrayed me.

The strangest part was the timing. The more we leaned into God, the more the world seemed to push back. It wasn't the "blessed" life I'd heard about in church; it was a season of being drained. Health, finances, family, everything felt like it was under a slow, steady pressure.

By the time we drove to Louisiana for Father's Day, we were empty. The drive was nothing but the sound of our own friction. We bickered until our feelings were raw, the kind of sharp, exhausted back-and-forth that makes you want to just turn the car around and give up on the weekend entirely. We finally decided to just have one last breakfast and call it a loss.

At the restaurant, I felt a strange pull toward the table next to us. It was like I could sense a frequency Eric couldn't. He heard them talking about running, the life we used to have. I heard them talking about God, the life we were struggling to lean more into.

When Eric told me God said to pay for their meal, my first instinct was to argue. I wasn't being a "good church girl." I was being the skeptic who hadn't heard a whisper from Heaven all morning. I told him he just wanted to be a nice guy, that if God was speaking, I was being left out of the conversation. I sat there in my own resistance, negotiating with the possibility that Eric was right and I was just closed off.

When he finally paid the bill, it felt like a door opening that I had been trying to keep shut. Meeting Keidra and holding her books felt heavy. I didn't read *Launch Out Into the Deep* for a year because I knew it was a call to leave the safety of the shallow end. I wasn't just resisting a book; I was resisting the realization that God was finally calling both of us at the same time.

I kept that book on my nightstand like a dare I wasn't ready to take. For a year, I looked at the cover and negotiated with the horizon, telling myself I was fine right where I was, injured, tired, and safely in the shallows. But you can only ignore a summons for so long before the weight of staying still becomes heavier than the risk of moving. Eventually, I had to stop being the girl who face-planted on the tile floor and start being the woman who was willing to get back up, even if I had to limp. That was the year the "stoic" version of Chris finally stayed behind in Louisiana, and the version of me that aligns with the Spirit started to take her first, shaky steps.

Whatever path I'm on now has given me more life than I have ever had before. I don't care if it's straight and narrow. I don't care if it looks restrictive to anyone else. The love, joy, peace, patience, kindness, goodness, faithfulness, gentleness, and long-suffering I carry with me every moment of my life now is priceless. It is worth every surrender, every tear, every hard lesson, every moment of unraveling that led me here.

I used to see that yellow suitcase and only see the tragedy of it. The brokenness. The 'multiple personalities.' But I've realized something important: mental illness isn't a death sentence. It's a thief, sure, but it didn't steal everything.

In her later years, despite her mind still fighting its battles, her spirit found a way to soar. She developed a relationship with God that was so real and so close, it makes my own faith look like a shadow. She taught me that God doesn't need a perfect mind to dwell in a person's heart.

It is the greatest irony of my life that the woman who was the most broken taught me more about the wholeness of God's love than anyone else in this world ever has. She showed me that God loves us in the mess, not just when we clean it up.

Looking back, I realize the yellow suitcase had been waiting for its own redemption long before it became my inheritance. For years, it sat in a shed behind her house, untouched and gathering dust, holding the weight of everything she used to be. But she had already moved past it. She had stopped journaling about the fifty-three versions of herself and started journaling about the only One who stayed the same.

I think that's where our stories finally overlap. I spent so long just trying to stay upright, trying to be as happy as possible before the clock ran out. I was managing an illusion and keeping my heart in a shed of my own making. But just like her, I finally stopped writing about the "Chris" I thought I had to be.

Having my own relationship with Jesus doesn't make the world perfect, my back still hurts, and the traffic is still heavy, but it makes the world make *sense*. I don't have to be the girl from the Sears catalog or the stoic widow who doesn't feel. I just have to be the one who finally walked into the shed, left the suitcase behind, and followed the sound of the Voice I first heard vibrating through my mother's chest.

This is the life I was meant to live as Chris. A carrier of Christ.

The End.

And the beginning of everything I never thought I'd have.

Unfiltered Grace

The following chapter is for everyone and especially anyone who has ever crossed my path. God made it all work together for good, just like He said He would. I know He's doing it for you too.

Peace.

HI ______________________!

(WRITE YOUR NAME HERE)

•♥•♥•♥•♥•♥•

Hey, how have you been? I've thought about you a lot lately. I know, how could I have been thinking about you when I don't even really know you right? I may not know everything about you, but you just read my book and I'm betting you probably found a part where you could have walked in my shoes a time or two.

Maybe you believe dreams are just something everybody else got when they grew up, but not you. Maybe you just didn't realize the reason your dream never came true was because you had been fighting your whole life to be a version of yourself that you weren't even supposed to be. I didn't know the reason I wrestled with God so long was because I wanted to be what I wanted to be AND who God created me to be.

> "But when it dies, God gives it a new form, a body to fulfill his purpose, and he sees to it that each seed gets a new body of its own *and becomes the plant he designed it to be.*" (1 Corinthians 15:38 TPT)

I was terrified to let God have control of my life. My kingdom. The safe bet was to build the best castle I could, with whatever I could get by working every minute I was awake. And let me tell ya, I built some pretty amazing castles.

The problem was, my feelings got hurt, a storm would come and the waves would wash away my sandcastle, and I would have to start over. They taught me about this in Sunday School. I didn't know the really meant me. That foolish man was me.

> "And everyone who hears these words of mine and does not do them will be like a foolish man who built his house on the sand. And the rain fell, and the floods came, and the winds blew and beat against that house, and it fell, and great was the fall of it." (Matthew 7:26-27 ESV)

I cannot tell you how many times I heard that story as a child. Enough that I have known the words by heart since I was very small and I have never forgotten them. I just wasn't good at the application process. My sandcastle fell and great was the fall of it.

I'm sure I don't have to tell you how it goes when you have everything all planned out and someone else comes and throws a big kink in your plans. Somehow, I got tricked into thinking that I was supposed to plan out my life and if I did a good enough job, I would be happy. I know I was tricked because God says this:

> "For I know the plans I have for you, declares the Lord, plans for welfare and not for evil, to give you a future and a hope." (Jeremiah 29:11 ESV)

He knows the plans, not me. But wait, there's more.

> "Then you will call upon me and come and pray to me, and I will hear you. You will seek me and find me, when you seek me with all your heart. I will be found by you, declares the Lord… (Jeremiah 29:12-14 ESV)

> "I will not disappoint you," declares Yahweh. "All that you have lost, I will restore, and I will regather you from all the nations where I have scattered you. I will bring you back home to the land from which I exiled you," declares Yahweh. (Jeremiah 29:14 TPT)

I wish I could reach through these words and sit beside you for a minute and try to explain how the hollow place in my soul was filled with a hope that turned into love beyond my understanding. I spent a lot of years living with my role and God's role reversed.

You've probably also spent a lot of your life trying to be what everyone else needed. Trying to be strong for everyone else. Keeping the peace. Being the dependable one. Playing the roles. Wearing the masks. You might have even tried to fulfill those "godly" expectations. And now, you're just… empty.

I don't know if you know this, but we are set apart. Separate. Not like the others.

> "But know that the Lord has set apart the godly for himself; the Lord hears when I call to him." (Psalm 4:3 ESV)

Wait. You are godly, right?

Because my mom used to remind me that the promise "everything works together for good" comes with the fine print "for those that love the Lord." And let me tell you, I spent a lot of years being the furthest thing from godly you can possibly imagine, but somehow, someway, God was always there and He did make everything work together for good anyway.

There were days I screamed at God. At least I thought I did, but Jesus reminded me,

> "No one comes to the Father except through Me." (John 14:6 ESV)

You don't think He understood what it felt like to be you? What about the time when

> "...overcome with grief, he threw himself down on the ground and prayed, "My Father, if there is any way you can deliver me from this suffering, please take it from me..." (Matthew 26:39 TPT)

Whenever I see those old, majestic oil paintings of Jesus in the wilderness, my brain always takes a weird turn. I picture him doing this overly dramatic, swoon to the ground, with the back of his hand on his forehead. But let us be real, what He was going through at that very moment was way worse than me locked in my bathroom ugly crying on my worst day. And even that messy visual does not touch the absolute chaos that had to be happening in his heart that day.

I know the chaos I feel in my own heart sometimes. It is one thing to be able to control what people see when you struggle. It is a completely different reality to actually live trying to keep that paralyzing, overwhelming weight in your chest hidden from everyone else. If you try to hide it and handle it on your own, you'll eventually crash into a wall where it is just all too much. Ask me how I know.

When it happens to me, I run. I don't even know where I'm going, I just know I cannot fight it without God and I run.

Jesus had at least twelve close friends. Friends that knew where he was almost at any given time. They made sure he was eating. They made sure he was safe. You would think they would have understood better than anyone how deep His despair was. They didn't have a clue.

The only One that truly understood what Jesus was going through was God. Jesus trusted God. Not just because God was His Father and Jesus was His Son and not even just because Jesus was God too, but I think more than anything it was because Jesus knew that God could be trusted. That's why Jesus was able to say:

> "...nevertheless, not as I will, but as you will." (Matthew 26:39 ESV)

Jesus knew exactly where He was headed. To die. You'd think knowing He was headed to the cross to be crucified would make me think less of myself and more about Him in my time of deep despair. No, my rebellious spirit would say *at least He knew where, when, why and how* and I would let myself sink deeper into my darkness.

I may not have been going to church, but I tried to be the best church girl with some exceptions that I just justified as being covered by grace. It was the worst year and the best year of my life. Then it was just a year I would think about occasionally. Then I pretty much forgot about that time of my life until I started writing this book and even then it would be forgotten and again brought back to my memory, this time to share.

> "Brothers, I do not consider that I have made it my own. But one thing I do: forgetting what lies behind and straining forward to what lies ahead," (Philippians 3:13 ESV)

I might not have been the best with doing what the rest of the book said to do, but that I did perfectly. If anyone would have asked my brother, he would have told them, "don't let her flip that switch. There's no going back once she does." The only problem was he's sometimes hard to understand, just like the Bible, no part of *don't let her* did he mean *when she gets to that point you have to stop her.* He knows that would be impossible.

There was a time I flipped the switch and not even my brother knew that would be the time I wouldn't want to rebuild my sandcastle. I would finally give up.

I really couldn't see my way out of it. Just a week prior, I was the owner of a very successful publishing business. I published telephone books. Remember those?! A week later, I would lose everything except the bills and my children. When I say everything, I literally mean I had a roof over my head, my children and all the bills. No utilities, no food, no job, no money, no nothing.

The one thing I still had that I couldn't seem to get rid of was my life.

The news station had been on my doorstep nearly every day. My entire life was spiraling out of control. I had been the responsible one. The one who was totally stone-cold sober all the time. I was the only one working, trying to pay the bills and providing for everyone else's needs, wants, and whims. There was no one else in this world that knew what I was dealing with. Nobody ever talked about anything like what was happening to me and I was so embarrassed that everyone else made life look so easy and *man, how dumb could I be.*

I can still feel the texture of the sheetrock against my back as I slid down my bedroom wall to land in a crumpled mess on the floor. I opened my hand and looked at the knife. Suddenly, startled by the phone ringing, I dropped the knife and answered the phone.

It was my mom. I started sobbing without any thought to how I looked, who was watching, what she would think or what I thought it would get me. I told her I was sorry I just couldn't do it anymore. It was just too hard. She hung up without saying goodbye. It was the one thing I couldn't get out of my mouth in time and I couldn't go knowing I didn't at least say goodbye to her. I knew she was on her way so I just sat there against the wall with my eyes closed and waited.

Somehow I was cocooned in a peace that soothed my soul that I hadn't felt in years. It should have taken her thirty minutes to get there, but somehow it only took her fifteen. She swooped in, gathered up me and my girls and marched us all out to her car, daring anyone to stop her.

As we left she admitted she told me, *you made your bed now you have to lay in it*, but God told her she was wrong. Nobody should have to lay in a bed like that while someone else watched and did nothing. Turns out she knew exactly what my bed was like because she had laid in the same one herself when she was my age.

She didn't want me to know. For a whole slew of valid reasons. One I could relate to was being under the pressure of trying not to screw up the life that you gave birth to, like your mom had screwed you up. Then there was the shame and the guilt because you turned around and did the same thing she did, just a little differently.

Over the next few weeks, in spite of losing everything, I gained my freedom. Some days were harder than others to face the world. At that time, the only hope I had was that if God really did love me, like my mom had assured me so often that He did in spite of everything I did, He would pull me out of it.

My mom called me one day and asked how long I had been laying on the couch. I remember thinking to myself *don't tell her the truth*. I told her I didn't know, but no matter how hard I tried, I just could not pull myself together and gather the motivation to get up off of it. I had been on that couch way longer than I wanted to admit.

I was barely getting by. It wasn't for lack of trying. The problem was I would get my hopes up and then get let down. I'd get my hopes up again and then get let down. I didn't trust anyone and I still didn't trust God. Even though I still believed in Him.

That particular day she said, "If all you can do is lay on that couch, then you just make sure you do that to the best of your ability and for the glory of God."

After we hung up, I laid there for a little while just puzzled. I wasn't even sure what that was supposed to mean. I decided why not try to follow the advice she was giving me even if it was kind of dumb. No doubt I was doing a great job of laying on the couch, but once I tried to literally follow her advice and lay there to the best of my ability and for the glory of God, I thought *this is dumb*. I gave up, got off the couch, and went and sat down at the piano. It was probably the best piece of advice she ever gave me.

I laid my Bible open on the keys and started reading it.

> "Out of the depths I cry to you, O Lord!" (Psalm 130:1 ESV)

God, if you really hear me, give me a song.

Over the next month or so, I carried a notebook and a pen with me everywhere I went. The words and the melody came at first like a trickle, then like a river. The day I knew the song was finished, I played it for my mom. I was convinced it was my song, but she would insist that it was her song. I didn't know it at the time, but she was right. It was her song.

> *Show them through me When they feel like giving up You're all they need. Show them through me Let me be a light so they can see.*

Here I am Like you said I'd be Crying for my father to come rescue me From this trouble That's blinded me Let thy will not mine be done, just quickly.

Peace, be still Rejoice and wait with me In my father's love and truth, He told me That my salvation Would comfort me It's peace that passes all my understanding.

More than anything in the world, she wanted people to know that if she of all people, in spite of the things she did and having a mental illness, could find favor with God, then there was no reason He would not extend His grace to anyone who would reach out and take it.

It would be easy to let you think that from that moment at the piano, my life was a perfect picture of faith and I was all in, but as I share in this book, that is not what happened at all. I got my freedom only to eventually put myself back in prison again. I wanted God, but I wanted Him on my own terms.

Ezekiel had a vision of a river flowing from God's temple. The water gets deeper and deeper until it requires complete surrender.

> "The behavior of the self-life is obvious: Sexual immorality, lustful thoughts, pornography, chasing after things instead of God, manipulating others, hatred of those who get in your way, senseless arguments, resentment when others are favored, temper tantrums, angry quarrels, only thinking of yourself, being in love with your own opinions,

> being envious of the blessings of others, murder, uncontrolled addictions, wild parties, and all other similar behavior..." (Galatians 5:19-21 TPT)

I learned the hard way that it is completely impossible to keep one foot securely in the self-life, while trying to fully surrender yourself in His river. You cannot do both. Not even in secret.

The reason I was so miserable is because we were made to be in the deep water.

> "Before I shaped you in the womb, I knew you intimately. I had divine plans for you before I gave you life, and I set you apart and chose you to be mine. You are my prophetic gift to the nations." (Jeremiah 1:5 TPT)

I know "set apart" sounds heavy and religious and your first thought is probably *she means He's talking about her*. No. I mean He is talking about *you*. You are the work of His hand. You are who He chose to be His. The reason you never felt like you fit in is because you don't. You have always known it. You are different. You are unique.

To realize just how unique, you have to know everything there is to know about God. And that's hard because how do you even begin to grasp all that encompasses the Omnipotent Holy God that is King of the whole universe? My mind cannot even begin to imagine his vastness. I've seen things with my own eyes that should be able to give me some idea of how big He is, but even my eyes cannot see.

> "...no eye has seen a God besides you, who acts for those who wait for him." (Isaiah 64:4 ESV)

When I walked out onto the overlook in the middle of the Grand Canyon, I felt the tiniest I had ever felt in my life and like all of God's attention, had suddenly zoomed in on just me all at the same time. It was almost too much for me to take in and it literally took my breath away.

I had imagined myself hollering into the canyon how much I loved Jesus and waiting to hear it echo back, but when I stood there in the middle of it all I could do was whisper *thank you for loving me this much.*

One of the surest things I know about Him is that it's because of how much He loves me and you, He gave us a piece of Himself in human form, so when we can't imagine Him as the Omnipotent Holy God that is King of the whole universe, we can imagine Jesus and what it might be like to look into His eyes and be held in his arms.

> "As one whom his mother comforts, so I will comfort you..." (Isaiah 66:13 ESV)

We all had to come from the descendants of Noah. I don't find it hard to believe that with all the wars and displacements and romances over the last 1900 years, it's possible that I could have come from the ordinary people that believed in Jesus and the Good News.

There had to be tens of thousands of them. He fed at least 10,000 of them on two different occasions. You know, my great, great, great all the way back. Yes, I believe I could be somebody's greatest grandchild. My heart skips a beat when I think that Jesus could have actually looked in the eyes of someone I came from.

What if He actually spoke to the one you came from? Those ordinary people that experienced His grace so close they could actually reach out and touch the hem of His robe. The ones in the Upper Room with the flames dancing above their heads. What if their faith in Jesus got bred into our DNA?

The tiniest seed of faith to believe that He lives in us.

> "Little children, you are from God and have overcome them, for he who is in you is greater than he who is in the world." (1 John 4:4 ESV)

AFTERWORD

Four years ago, when I first sat down to write this book, I was paralyzed.

I had let so much time pass before I finally tried to tell her story. Every time I opened a notebook, all I could think about was what I might have forgotten. I worried that I wasn't remembering things right. I was terrified that I wasn't telling her story the way *she* wanted it told.

That is when I opened an old box of journals and found the answer.

Inside, buried among the memories, I found a CD I had made for her years ago—a recording of my song. Written on the face of the CD in marker were three words:

Chris Show Them

It felt like a message reaching out from the past to guide my future. My hands shook as I put it in the player. I wondered if it was just the song, or if she was telling me exactly what I was supposed to do. *Show them.*

With the CD, there was a folded-up piece of paper she had written on. It was a list of promises she must have clung to, and now, they were promises for me to cling to:

I am Your God. I will go before you and I will be with you. I will never leave you. Do not be discouraged. Do not be afraid. (Deut. 31:8)

And after you have suffered for a little while, the God of all grace who called you to his eternal glory in Christ will Himself perfect, confirm, strengthen and establish you. (1 Peter 5:10)

The Lord is my light and my salvation—whom shall I fear? The Lord is the stronghold of my life—of whom shall I be afraid? (Ps. 27:1)

For you did not receive a spirit that makes you a slave again to fear, but you received the spirit of sonship. And by Him we cry, "Abba, Father." (Rom. 8:15)

When you pass through the waters, I will be with you; and through the rivers, they shall not overflow you. When you walk through the fire, you shall not be burned, nor shall the flame scorch you. For I am the Lord your God. (Isaiah 43:2-3)

She lived in fear in one form or another her whole life. The fear of people finding out about her multiple personalities. The fear of people not liking her. The fear of what people would think. The fear of not being able to love, and the fear of not being loved.

When I wrote that song, she told me she knew it was *her* song because so many times she thought she was in the pits of Hell and wanted to give up. She said that if just one person could see that she came out okay because God carried her through it, then they would know God could carry them, too.

I promised her I would sing this song at her funeral, and I did.

And I promised that if I ever found this recording, I would share it.

It took four years to get here, but I finally kept that promise. And fortunately, after all this time, the CD still played.

Journal Entries

The following are journal entries written by my mom that might shed a little more light on her situation. It helped me to understand a little more about her. All of the different pieces of her.

I started the day in a pretty good place. Betty and I talked this morning. I felt she had peace because we connected. I told her that I had to work today and that she probably would not have fun there so she could go to a safe fun place. She wanted me to take the playpen along and so I did, but she knew that I was planning on spending time with her later. I really wasn't sure what would be fun for her. I felt that things she shared this morning about her feelings were valid. They are things I can't write about when other people are around. So I thought we should write about them now. There is an inner child who seems to think that I will die soon. This fearful one needs to know I will not die. No I won't. Now I understand you are afraid for me. It is okay to feel what you feel, but stop telling me over and over will you. This fear you have is not my problem. It is your problem and when I can talk more about it to you I will. It is now Betty's turn. If this child who is so afraid is Betty or one of Betty's friends or playmate, Betty may want you to share now. If

not we're going to talk about what you are so afraid of later. My Inner Child has a story she wants to tell. Her story is a picture with words. A Shepherd with sheep and a staff and a rod. He leads and they follow. But should they miss the direction His staff is quick to pull them in and His rod they may feel on their behinds. But mercy and goodness are in this Shepherd's heart and as a loving Shepherd who would even die for His sheep He cares for them. I want to name my sheep, but it is hard at this point to really know who is who. Perhaps a good way to express my picture is to say I feel each one of these sheep are a part of my soul. But each one seems capable of going it's own way. I want each one to know it is loved, just as it is. I chose to love each one just as they are. I'm at the point that I believe they have believed some lies. They think their lies a'e truth and truth is a lie. So we need individual attention for each one. And I think my Shepherd must really have His hands full. I feel guilty He has such a big job, a'd a little angry that this job is there for Him to do. Yet I want to get over the anger cause I see the need for His help is crucial. His lamb (sheep) that lets shame cover her, I want her to know that she does not have to let shame cover her anymore. It is her habit to accept shame and this is sad. It keeps her from the good warm love feelings she deserves. Not because she's earned but because of who she belongs to.

12-24-96 6:55 a.m.Dear Journal,There's no way to decide what I should write about first. Today is Christmas Eve. I'll be taking care of Andrea this morning and running alot of errands. I'm going to stop and write these out now. There, now I won't forget. It has been an okay 3 days. I'm not sure who is out.

I said 3 days because I'm not sure when I journaled last. I've gained some weight, and it really bothers me. However, I'm trying to get myself to see this could be an exercise to practice not condemning myself. Whenever I think there needs to be a behavior change, the old belief system is to start condemning myself til I feel bad enough to do something about it.But you see that is just it. It is an old belief system that I don't think I need to use anymore. It never worked in the past with good results so why do I want to use it now. Other coping systems such as denial want to kick in then. Pretend you are not fat. Feel the extra gaudy fat between your legs, sit down, oh you are not fat, walk, feel the extra gaudy fat between your legs. The system is really divided on this issue. I don't really think it is the most important thing there is to write about but ...... I've learned to listen. Okay. Open house. Everyone is entitled to an opinion. I know I've been really ignoring you and I am sorry. Let's talk about the fat. ***How we look is important.*** Why?***People judge you by how you look.*** Should they do that? Is that our problem?***If we don't watch out we'll be as fat as Donna.*** Right. Agree.

12-24-96 cont. 7:35 a.m.Andrea is not coming. Have mixed feelings about it. Told Chris she would be responsible for her broken heart if she has one. Broken hearts. Little children. We could keep our lives in an unmanageable state if we dwelled on that. Let's get centered again, we all know the way to help little children most is by doing our own inventories. Back to the fat talk. Question for the one who says, "this extra fat is so disgusting."What's disgusting? Donna or looking like Donna. Are we afraid to look like Donna because we will be disgusting

like Donna or what?*I don't want to look like Donna.* That is okay that you feel that way. I'm wanting to give you a break. You can feel what you feel and not be ashamed. Let's be honest about what we feel.Here's another thought that I think I hear when we walk, and we feel this extra fat between our legs. Isn't it reminding someone about what Jackie said about Tina? In fact, I've got an idea that this extra fat is triggering some new altars or provoking some silent altars to talk that have been mostly quiet before. I have an altar (at least one) who thinks in pictures. This thing about Jackie and Tina has been like a picture thought, and then I feel ...... a cringe, you know ... the picture and then while it's going on a cringing .. disgust .. then struggle with denial ..... then say we're going to do something about this ... then realize we can't right now ....*This is so stupid, you are spending valuable time writing about stupid stuff.*You feel what you feel and it's okay.This is kind of like the clothing problem. And even though some people may not understand about that, Kenna for one said that was not stupid. If we were in group today and telling her about his, again .... she for one would not say this is stupid. In fact she would say, "This is not stupid." And I think she is going to be proud of me for listening to all of you about this. How we feel about the fat is very important. *Compulsive overeating is a form of denial, what about the program, what about addictions, what are you going to do?*As much as I want to not go to any of the OA meetings, I'm beginning to think we are going to have to. I am just not able to work the program without at least one meeting a week. Thurs. and Sat. are our only options. And we really dislike some of the people who come to these meetings. (She reminds us of Donna.) Everyone's in an uproar about Donna. All I said was I wanted to work on not being jealous of her. There's an expression that comes to mind, but the altar that thinks in pictures is really working today. Maybe she/he is out. Just alot of things are visual today. I've been thinking about adding some new stuff to my book. And it's all coming as pictures. Belief system city I guess you'd call it. Draw a map with streets marked wide enough to write on. Call those streets by name, and their names could be things like Condemnation, Shame, I Can't Believe You Think Things Like That. Different belief systems that if I let myself dwell on them they lead me to ---depression, big hole---, there could be alleys and little paths around that have similar names that if followed you'd still end up in the big hole that each street has on it. Of course, we need a super highway. This one could have new belief systems that we want to incorporate into our new self, or replace for the old self as she/he is willing to let them go. It's like, some people take all kind of city streets to get to the airport, and some people get on 440 and get right out there with no hassle, little traffic and few traffic lights. But sometimes all those exits mislead you and you take the wrong one and before you know it you are in a wrong belief system again. Not only is depression there but "acting out" and who knows what all the things that happen because you are back on those "old" belief systems again. However, we are where we are. It's kind of like feelings. I got to accept the feelings before I can do anything about them. Same way with belief systems which are actually connected to a great deal of feelings. Back to our topic.Being fat brings up all kinds of belief systems about the subject. Until we gained this last 7 lbs. our legs didn't wiggle this much when we walked and it wasn't hard to cross our legs and all this stuff wasn't being triggered.For today, I think the altar that is out is most concerned with the "Jackie and Tina" thing. Maybe Donna too. I want to write something to this altar who's getting the Jackie picture every time I walk. Jackie's belief system was that fat people were a disgrace. Jackie's belief system was wrong. There is not one real reason for fat people to feel ashamed or feel that they are a disgrace. Also, we aren't going to get much help from the others to lose weight if we are going to hear you say in a sense "do it for her." Her being Jackie. I can't think of any of us that want to do anything for her. Yet you are so concerned about what she said about fat legs. So.....so she doesn't like fat legs. That is her problem. We might as well accept that we are going to have fat legs for at least 30 days. That would be the absolute quickest, with diet and 20 minutes of exercise every day except one day a week. Now are we going to hate ourselves for 30 days? I hope not. Come on. Let's give ourselves a break. We can get on a food plan. We can work the program, but most of all we can like ourselves while we do it. I like me. All _____ however many there are of me. I'm thankful for healthier altars who can help me love and support those who are still on those city streets, "old belief systems". We can love them while they are there, and as soon as they want help getting out of there let's help them. We've got a super highway that's really grand. It doesn't believe you are ever separated from the love of God. Don't you all want to come and get on it? And

all the altars said..... some are still hiding from love say.... and some who know love is what always needed say.... and some just don't know what to say. But that's okay, shepherd, please lead the way.

12-26-96 8:15 a.m.

Dear Journal,

I think I should draw a picture....

8:30 a.m.

I'm not sure what this picture means. I know it describes a message from my inner child. I think it's Linda. I feel she wants to talk internally but studders. If she could go ahead and talk even though she studders it would be okay with me.

Daddy hurt me on the couch. Baby go to sky. He make my baby go to sky.

How could he do that? What are you talking about? I want to understand. I ask for help from my Higher Power to help me accept Truth. Even if it scares me. Please inner child help me understand truth. Are babies, dolls to you? Did your doll go to the sky? Can you tell me how old you are when this happened? How old are you in this picture?

Her baby go to sky. I make her baby go to sky.

Whose baby? Whose baby go to sky?

Mommies, if she crys.

I'm not sure what's going on here, but we are feeling some intense feelings now. And a smell and feel of a brown couch......and darkness and a fear of making mommy cry and sexual feelings and having to suppress crying from pain. And alot of.......intense stuff.

12-26-96 9:00 a.m.

Dear Journal,

What I want to do now is tell myself that I feel what I feel and it is okay. I can not remember what you just told me happened to you, but I believe you anyway. Because you feel what you feel and I care. What I want you to know is that I am trying very hard to believe that what you just told me really happened. We can't do much more until I do. When we were talking to God and you showed me this picture, were you perhaps wanting Him to know about this? Could it be that you had something you wanted to talk to Him about that had to do with the picture? Feelings are really important. I want you to share your feelings and pictures with me. You don't have to worry about getting into trouble. We have a Higher Power who does not spank you for feelings. Maybe your need for pictures helps you handle your feelings. Maybe your feelings are where your pictures come from. As you share more with me I will begin to understand better what is going on with you and why you feel what you feel.

If you have more things you want to talk to me about this morning I am willing to listen. We can talk about your feelings or pictures. I think you should plan on letting another altar come out when we go to work. There's much to much for you to do there in the store and you don't need to work so hard. I want you to stay in a safe place while I go to work, but not go there now. Your safe place is a closet. If you feel safe there then that is okay for you to stay there. I'm glad you have come out today to talk to me. We are friends. What do you like to do? Do you like to color or draw pictures?

I just remembered, Robert had said he had bought us some paper dolls, we thought. I know we had pictured them and how we were going to play with them. Maybe he meant he was going to buy them. Also he didn't buy the Therapy aroma stuff that he said he was going to get us. We probably shouldn't have said anything about this to him but it is hard isn't it when you've pictured something as yours and then they say, now it isn't here. It makes you feel like it is something that you had but it got taken away, don't it? Well, see I am beginning to understand. The aroma therapy stuff ---- now you can't do that ---- you feel sad. You are wondering if we should buy some with the money Mrs. Kelly gave you, that would be pampering. Let's not forget that we can send off for Many Voices now.

I think we should open this up for all voices to talk awhile. I know I've been keyed in on Linda and an altar who speaks and feels pictures. But I can sense some others who'd like to talk about some stuff. Going to take a break and then come back. Keep those feeling and thoughts coming.

12-26-96 9:40 a.m.

Dear Journal,

I know that there are alot of feelings and thoughts that need to be validated. Let's just be free for awhile and acknowledge them.

My oldest son. Did we do a bad thing? He probably is really hurt because he didn't get a present for Christmas. Every time I think about it I feel like many voices come up and want to think about it. I feel like many voices come up and want to say how they feel. So each need to take a turn. Remember this is a safe place to feel what you feel and it is okay. And I as the host am not sure we or I chose the right or appropriate action. It just kind of happened.

My oldest son is very content to buy his own self everything his heart desires. Because he has shared with me/us that he has bought this and this and this and this --for himself-- but said "no, I didn't buy anything for you." We chose not to give him anything Christmas day. Now I'm not sure why we did that when we know that he was expecting about a $15.00 something. When we were trying to figure out what to get him for Christmas and asking for hints. We said, keep it in the $15.00 range. Now personally, I don't like my whole method of giving presents. Maybe this year since we are more open to listen to all the conflicting opinions of each different altar, we can come up with a more suitable method of giving.

I think some embrace ideas from our abusers. Evidently a gift was somehow, at least once, connected to an abuse. And what to give to someone for a present, doesn't seem like a joyful adventure but one of extreme potential danger. One of us at least views this gift giving adventure as a devious deed. And really really wishes people never ever had the custom of giving presents to each other at least on Christmas. Birthdays, that is a much more important time.

Shame and gift giving. I'd like to talk to some altars who have felt ashamed when they were given a gift or gave a gift. I imagine there were alot of you who were exposed to shame when gift giving was a concern. Well, I want to tell you something. Gift giving or gift receiving or not giving is not a shame. Whoever thinks it is has a right to feel that way about it. Whatever happened to cause you to feel that way was a valid experience I'm sure. I want to hear about these experiences. But, just like the little girl who said "yes to shame" instead of getting a spanking, we can learn a new way to respond to gift giving and receiving if we work together. People -up now- have to close.

12-28-96 7:25 a.m.

Dear Journal,

Yesterday I decided that I needed to give my Christmas present from Chris, back. If I don't type my reasons I may forget and a new altar may not even understand. So far the only conflict in the system has been how to deal with Robert when you tell him.

I feel that some are thinking the conflict with him is going to be worse than any conflict and without his support can we do it? Do we have enough strength? And this is why I've decided to spend some time before the Lord with this matter. Because if this indeed is the right thing to do, I feel He'll give me the strength I need to do it. But there are those in the system who are not very sure about that. Some have seen me try to do what is right before and have a really hard time with Robert, and do the wrong thing where Robert was concerned, making my right a wrong.

So let's back up a little bit. Reason to give gift back. I have 3 grown children. One did not give me a present because it is all he can do to keep his car, his concert tickets bought, his life style going that he and his friends enjoy and so on. Not even a card, or a dollar present.

One is also facing hard times, he can buy all kinds of stuff needed for a hunting trip, and put out $100.00 for a good buy on a (second) guitar, but that is all he can do to keep himself going. No card, no present.

One bought me a present. Well, actually her live in boyfriend bought it. But had she bought it, the reason would be the same for giving it back. She and I had a conversation right after she had chosen to live with this male friend. Her reason for doing this was not love. It was so she would not be poor. This point was made clear to me when she called me and told me that I had hurt her feelings because I had suggested the alternative to living with him, and accept being poor. It was as if I'd told her to go to jail or something. And she really did not like it. I had pointed out how we had not remained poor when I had chosen a life of being a single mother and remaining moral. (Because I did not date). That after two years we had come into enough money to buy a house and so on. And even when we lived in a trailer with holes in the floor, we had food and were able to avoid the public schools and go to private school.

But she said, "All she could remember was the holes in the floor and living in the trailer". In other words she feared ending up like that and rather than take the risk she has chosen to live with a male friend.

I had took a stand of sorts and said I would not come to visit her. This was right. But it had not occurred to me how double standard it was for me to do that but still accept presents from her. Presents she might not be able to afford to give had she not chosen a life of immorality. So I wish to give her present back. And I will.

Well, I stopped and went in and talked to Robert about it. He understood and there was no problem. I realized that he wouldn't have a problem with it after I wrote about it and I was right.

Also I shared with him some of my feelings about gift giving for next year.

So now I guess I should dump those out. Mainly, I'd like there to be freedom when I give. And to give to those people in my life that partake in this holiday and chose to exchange presents. It seems to me that I am a foreigner in a strange land. And that going along with the Christmas custom is kind of like the Bible tells us, about where it talks about should your brother eat vegetables, don't insist that it's okay to eat your meat if it's going to make him stumble. For me this is what I've done finally. Is say I understand this is your way of showing Jesus He is special by doing as He showed us --- and gave --- so we give. However, if you are not a participant of this holiday, should you give, but give only to those who've chosen to celebrate this way? I see nothing wrong next year to give to those who give. And I'm going to suggest to Chris that she make me a present. Because she is very craft able to do that well even on her own. In fact when I give her present back I may suggest that she give me a craft type present if she desires to do so. Now that we've gotten past worrying about how Robert will respond we need to think about how Chris will respond. And how to respond to her in a healthy way.

12-30-96

Dream.

I was in a Bible store. New to me. With a child. We waited for people to stop talking amongst themselves before they waited on us. Then I named off three things I wanted to buy. I saw her write them down. (Even thought I saw words. It seems strange to me. I cannot read them or tell you what they are, nor what I wanted, it was as if in code.) We are at a counter and the little girl beside me says, "remember you want to buy another Bible, just like mine". Immediately one is brought to the counter in front of us. I pick it up and say "I think I'll wait on this, I didn't tell you, (little girl) but I think I've decided to look at others. The lady at the counter wants to put a nameplate on it. She says that she too had thought of looking at other Bibles, but those that put things in categories are best. She pulls out a silver looking nameplate to fasten to the side of the Bible. I say okay, this is what I'll get.

12-31-96 7:20 p.m.

Dear Journal,

Betty's been with me today. She is very interesting. My new hairstyle is her choice. I took time to make it look good this morning. I also wrote about a dream I had. I can't seem to get interested in any books about how to read dreams. I figured the first step is to start recording an inner child that I'm interested in what's trying to be said. I think maybe I feel approval from some inner child when I write down my dreams.

Today I thought of letters to write and articles for magazines to write and things to add to my book. Tonight I just want to write. I love to write. It is more fun than anything else I get to do. I like to write. Someone will read it some day and some one will know I am here and I feel.

Me too, Mom. Me too.

www.ingramcontent.com/pod-product-compliance
Lightning Source LLC
LaVergne TN
LVHW100523110826
845146LV00002B/751

* 9 7 9 8 9 9 5 4 9 2 9 1 7 *